The Aficionado's

SOUTHWESTERN
COOKING

The Aficionado's Southwestern Cooking

By Ronald Johnson

Decorations by
Louie Ewing

UNIVERSITY OF NEW MEXICO PRESS

Contents

Introduction   vii

Ingredients & Methods   3

Appetizers   9

Fish   15

Eggs   20

Soups   24

Meat   31

Poultry   40

Barbecues   44

Tamale Pies   48

Dishes Using Tortillas   53

Beans & Rice   70

Vegetables   78

Salads   86

Sauces   97

Desserts   102

Menus   114

Index   119

 *Introduction*

These recipes are as old as the Aztecs and as new as yesterday, for Mexican cooking in the Southwestern United States, though imported from below the border via Spain, is our only continuing indigenous cuisine. The rest is only a sprinkling of Indian puddings and succotash.

Most of the plants grew here, either wild, or cultivated by the Indians, when the settlers arrived: principally corn, chile and beans—but there were wild herbs too, and pumpkins, squashes, persimmons, piñons. . . on and on. The ingredients still remain, but with new methods the cuisine has grown and changed. If you visit a home in New Mexico or Arizona you will find delicious and subtle chile dishes (for chiles should never, or seldom, be used merely as pitchforks in taste-buds, but for flavor—and chiles are also one of the finest natural digestives in the world). You may have the newest cold avocado soup whirled in a modern blender or a succulent pork loin roasted with chiles, bacon, oranges and bananas which could have been prepared centuries ago. You will also find that the enchiladas are as varied as apple pies, and as with apple pies, home-cooked are best.

I have used English for Spanish throughout, except where the

Spanish word has become part of the language. But you may wish to say frijoles for beans, or salsa for sauce, as they often do in the Southwest. Also you will find that the ingredients here are those which can be found nearly anywhere from Mystic, Connecticut, to Muncie, Indiana—and beyond.

It is the custom in some homes and most restaurants to serve a platter of enchiladas, tacos, etc., refried beans and Mexican rice. However, in the menus I have suggested there is only one that is typical of this practice, since the choice is wide and everyone has his favorite combination. The discriminating will find that Mexican food can adapt itself to the satisfying pauses of courses, rather than being heaped altogether on a plate, both bewildering and indigestible. The best meals come in variations of texture, flavor, and heat, in an ordered succession. The good cook will take the extra time to consider the progression of a meal, and not leave everything to random forks. And if you love Mexican food as I do, you will be able to serve it more often if you choose from a whole variety of dishes.

As a rule the best beverage to drink with Mexican food is beer and, if it is available, Mexican beer is excellent. Wine is at a disadvantage with hotter spices such as curry and chile, but it would not be out of place to serve wines with many of the dishes included here—a full-bodied white wine with Trout Frosted with Guacamole, or Chicken with Pumpkin Seed Sauce, for instance, or the same dry red wine you have used to cook the Leg of Lamb in Chile Wine Sauce.

Like any cuisine, Mexican food is based on certain ingredients, methods, sauces, etc., which, once mastered, make the preparation of food fast and simple. I always keep in the refrigerator the ingredients for Cooked Green Chile Sauce, and a fresh bottle of Cold Green Chile Sauce, and frozen containers of Chile Meat Sauce. A pot of cooked pinto beans will keep for a week or more if refrigerated. Tortillas should always be as fresh as possible. From a limited variety of ingredients it is possible to cook many dishes: for instance you will find that the Chile Meat Sauce can immediately become Chile Con Carne with the addition of pinto or kidney beans, or can top Huevos Rancheros, enchiladas, meatloaf or hamburgers, and can combine with practically anything for tacos or tostadas. Many of these dishes can be served with other foods which are not indigenously Mexican. A good steak broiled and topped before serving with cold Guacamole could be served with a baked potato or Gratin de Pommes de Terre as well as with tortillas and beans. Tacos can take the place of sandwiches any day, and there are many dishes here which, if you have the basic sauces on hand, can be made into an interesting meal as quickly as anything but a T.V. 'Dinner.'

The gourmet will find that Mexican food offers both surprises and delights. A properly prepared Puree of Garbanzos is as distinguished as a chestnut puree, as well as being cheaper and more easily prepared. Many of the dishes here appear exotic at the first reading and make one want to rush to the market for the ingredients. But I cannot describe to you, nor does it show on the page, the ineffable odors coming from a slowly cooked Baked Pork Loin with Oranges, nor tell you, till you taste it, what a rich delight is Guacamole served on steak, cold roast beef—or even hamburgers. I have served, with inevitable success, Scrambled Eggs with Tortillas and Eggs with Chorizo to the most discriminating, and what could be more simple? The avocado is at its most unexpected in Avocado Ice Cream. And the delicacy of Chicken Crepes with Green Chile Sauce. . . . I can only say I wish you as much joy cooking and eating as I have had in preparing this book.

THE RECIPES

Ingredients and Methods

A v o c a d o s : These may be used after they just begin to feel soft, but for desserts I find they are best when quite ripe. They darken quickly after being peeled, but lemon juice squeezed over the flesh, or the seed of the avocado left in the bowl (the bowl should always be covered) will delay the darkening process.

B e a n s : There are many excellent beans used in Mexico which are unheard of and unavailable in this country. Pinto beans and kidney beans are the most common varieties here, and both are used, often interchangeably, in the Southwest. Canned beans of either variety may be substituted in any recipe here, but they are never equal to dried beans cooked slowly for a day or more. Their flavor may be enhanced, however, by cooking them with a small onion, a slice of bacon, and perhaps a clove of garlic and a pinch of chili powder. I also find the commercial canned black bean soup an interesting addition in flavor to many bean recipes, either diluted with water or simply as it comes from the can. By all means experiment with it in your cooking—it seems no longer to be stocked in some stores, but your grocer will order it for you if you request it. Garbanzos, or chick peas, may also be considered beans, and are used in many ways in the Southwest. As with pinto or kidney beans, dried beans you have cooked yourself are preferable to canned. These take very long slow cooking, but should be still a bit *al dente* rather than mushy when you serve them.

C H E E S E : The two cheeses I find best suited to Mexican cooking are the mild Monterey Jack and a sharp cheddar, but there are many cheeses to choose from and to substitute. I do not recommend, however, Longhorn cheese since it is often too green when it comes to the market and tends toward strands of taffy when cooked. Never, of course, use processed "American Cheese." Though it may melt easily and is "mild," it has a flavor which can permeate a whole dish, overpowering even the pungencies of chile, so that the best of enchiladas become redolent of drugstore counters.

C H I L E S : Chiles, like beans, come in many varieties in Mexico. Even in the Southwest you will find many more than I have used in this book, but everywhere you will be able to find, if not fresh green chiles, at least canned ones—pickled jalapeño peppers—and, of course, chili powders and Tabasco sauce, etc.

GREEN CHILES: These are called *poblano chiles* and must be roasted and peeled before using. To prepare fresh green chiles place on a shallow pan under the broiler and keep turning as they puff up and blister. When they are completely blistered remove from the pan and let them steam covered in a damp towel. When they are cooled the skin slips off easily. Remove the stems and also the seeds and any veins clinging to the inside. The chiles may be frozen before peeling. Canned green chiles are ready to use as is.

RED CHILES: In the Southwest these are dried in the sun and often hung in strings against the house, or inside on the walls, then ground to powder when needed or made into red chile paste which may be frozen. Ground red chile can also be purchased in packets but it is often more "heat" than flavor, so make sure it is fresh when you buy it.

4

JALAPEÑO CHILES: These are very, very hot, but I have found one or two varieties of them which are *comparatively* mild and have used them throughout this book—so be guided accordingly when using them!

CHILI POWDER: Use the best possible you are able to buy, it will be well worth the extra money. My favorite is Spice Islands Chili Powder.

CHILI SAUCES: These come green, red, hot, mild, good or indifferent. A good one may be used to add hotness or varied flavor to dishes. Find one you like, and experiment with it.

TABASCO SAUCE: Tabasco can pick up the flavor of nearly any mild dish, and once you are used to using it for flavor rather than for mere hotness you will find it, as most Southwestern cooks do—as necessary as salt and pepper.

CHORIZO: This is the Mexican sausage. It is often available in the markets, but even when it is I prefer to use the recipe for chorizo used in this book as it is quite easily prepared and has a much better flavor than the commercial variety. If you are using "store-bought," however, where I indicate here to use *crumbled chorizo*, simply remove the sausage stuffing from the cases and proceed.

GARLIC: When I indicate *pressed cloves of garlic* I mean garlic that has been put through a garlic press. Very finely minced garlic, however, does as well.

GREEN PEPPERS: I have often, in these recipes, used *grated green pepper*. To do this simply slice the pepper in quarters and remove the stem and seeds, then grate on the smallest blade of your grater, skin outward so the flesh is grated but you have the skin left. This will be much easier than roasting them and peeling them as you do green chiles. For those who believe green peppers must always

5

be indigestible, this will be an amazement, since the indigestible part is the skin. If you are only able to find canned green chiles, also, you will find fresh green peppers added to the green chiles an improvement in flavor.

LAMB'S-QUARTERS: This plant is neglected in most of the country, but throughout the West and Midwest it is gathered as the best of wild spring greens. In the Southwest it is known locally as *quelites*, and it is in the goosefoot family. In Mexico it is commonly used in the preparation of all bean dishes—I recommend it highly in this way. Unless I am mistaken some is growing either in your yard or in the vacant lot next door. It grows quickly, and after it becomes more than a foot high it is no longer as succulent for cooking as spring greens, but it can be used until it flowers for cooking as a potherb, and if you have a patch of it you can keep pinching off the beginning flowers in order to use the plant all summer long.

MASA HARINA: This is the corn flour from which tortillas and tamales are made. You will find it in any specialty store, where it also sometimes comes as *Masa*, which is the flour to which water has been added to make a paste ready to use.

MSG: Monosodium glutamate—it brings out the natural flavors of foods.

ONIONS: Any variety of onion may be used, as you please, when it is to be cooked. But many of these recipes call for raw onion and I find the usual yellow or white onions are rather harsh for this. Green spring onions, or Spanish onions, are much sweeter and milder and do not overpower the dish in which they are eaten raw. If these are not available, soak the onion, sliced thinly or chopped, in cold salt water for half an hour or more, then drain and substitute for spring onions, etc., in any dish they are called for.

6

PEPITAS: These are toasted pumpkinseeds and are available now in most stores.

PIÑON NUTS: These "pine nuts" are gathered all over the Southwest and are sold both unshelled and shelled. However, to shell them is quite a task, and most health food stores sell the shelled nuts.

SQUASH BLOSSOMS: These are used more often in Mexico, but were used also by the early residents of the Southwest. If you have a patch of squash in your garden they are well worth bringing back, and they lend an exotic air to any dinner. The blossoms to use are the male which drop off the vine anyway. In order to determine this you must pick before 10:00 in the morning as sun closes the flowers later.

TAMALES AND TAMALE PIES: I have included no recipes for tamales here as they are too time consuming to be convenient for most modern cooks. I have, however, given several recipes for Tamale Pie fillings and Masa 'mixtures' which can be used interchangeably.

TOMATILLO: These are small green tomatoes used fresh in Mexico, but are only available in this country canned. Our green tomatoes are no substitute, however, for tomatillo is entirely another variety.

TOMATOES: I find that when you are to use tomatoes in most cooked dishes, canned ones are better than those offered in the markets during the winter. Canned tomatoes are picked at their height, while, except in the summer, fresh tomatoes now have the consistency and flavor of plastic. In dishes calling for the tomatoes to be raw they should always be peeled first, then seeded. To peel a tomato simply place it in boiling water for a minute or so. Remove and when it is cool enough to handle the skin will slip off easily.

TORTILLAS: Both corn and flour tortillas are available nearly everywhere now—long gone are the days when cookbooks must give a recipe for dubious substitutes calling for cornmeal. If you are not lucky enough to have access to fresh tortillas, or even frozen ones, there are always canned ones. Frozen tortillas are excellent, generally (though beware: I have found several times some "pre-fried" ones which are inexcusable) but they should be thawed before using. They will keep in the refrigerator without drying for almost a week. I do not recommend trying to make your own corn tortillas unless, however, you have Indian blood. Tortillas are usually fried crisp or soft. The recipe for Cocktail Tostadas indicates the method for crisp frying which is used for tacos, tostadas, etc. Where I indicate the tortillas should be fried 'lightly' this means the tortilla should be fried in medium hot fat on both sides until it just softens and begins to puff up.

Appetizers

COCKTAIL TOSTADAS

1 tb. salt   1 doz. tortillas   ½ cup water hot fat

Cut the tortillas in eighths. Dissolve the salt in the water and sprinkle over the tortillas. Let them stand until nearly dry, then cook in hot fat until gold and crisp. Drain on absorbent paper.

Note: Test the fat first with one tostada—when the fat stops bubbling it will be done, but if the tostada is more brown than gold by this time, the fat is too hot.

VARIATIONS

Cook the tortillas as above, but cut them into quarters rather than eighths. Spread with any of the following:

Refried beans; then sour cream mixed with minced, peeled green chiles; then Parmesan cheese.

Fried crumbled chorizo; then softened cream cheese; then sliced ripe olives.

Guacamole (see p. 87); then chopped lettuce (or toasted piñon nuts, or pepitas, or bits of fried bacon).

Grated sharp cheddar; then a sprinkling of chili powder: Put in hot oven until the cheese is melted and serve immediately.

Softened cream cheese mixed with ground walnuts; then a strip of green chile; then Parmesan cheese.

COCKTAIL TOSTADAS WITH CHILI POWDER

Make cocktail tostadas as above, and when they have drained on absorbent paper, shake them in a paper bag with chili powder.

BEAN DIPS

NUMBER ONE

4 cups cooked pinto beans (see p. 70)
2 tb. bacon fat
garlic salt, to taste

1 tb. Worcestershire sauce
3-4 pickled jalapeño peppers, seeded and minced

Put drained pinto beans through a food mill and add the rest of the ingredients along with enough liquid from the cooked beans to make the puree the consistency of very thick cream. Keep the bean dip hot in a chafing dish, and serve with cocktail tostadas. Serves 6-8.

Note: If you wish, 1 cup of grated cheese may be added to the beans.

NUMBER TWO

1 cup refried beans (see p. 71)
1 cup sour cream
salt to taste

Jalapeño sauce (see p. 101)
to taste

Prepare refried beans and when they are just beginning to acquire a brown crust add the sour cream and salt. Cook slowly until the mixture is heated through, then add as much Jalapeño sauce as desired. Serve hot in a chafing dish with cocktail tostadas. Serves 4-6.

COLD GARBANZO

1 lb. dried garbanzos
1 cup minced onion
3 tb. olive oil

1 pressed clove of garlic
2 tb. minced parsley
2 tb. piñon nuts

Soak garbanzos overnight, then boil until tender. Drain and put through a food mill. Sauté the onions until transparent in olive oil with the garlic and parsley. Add the piñon nuts and sauté a few minutes more. Add to the garbanzos and mix thoroughly. Salt to taste. Serve cold with cocktail tostadas. Serves 6-8.

PICKLED JALAPEÑOS
STUFFED WITH WALNUT CHEESE

1 3-oz. package of cream cheese　salt to taste
⅓ cup ground walnuts　pickled jalapeño peppers

Cream the cream cheese with walnuts and salt. Remove the stems and seeds from the peppers and stuff with the cheese mixture. Refrigerate for several hours, or until the cheese has become firm, then remove and slice into very thin rings. Serves 4-6.

MEXICAN CASHEWS

2 cups cashew nuts　¼ tsp. powdered red chile
1½ tbs. butter　½ tsp. each ground cumin and
1 tsp. salt　coriander

Sauté the cashew nuts in butter for several minutes, then remove to drain on absorbent paper. Place the salt, powdered chile, and spices in a paper bag and shake until the nuts are well coated.

RIPE OLIVES
STUFFED WITH GREEN CHILE

1 can ripe pitted olives　¼ tsp. dried oregano
¼ cup olive oil　1 pressed clove of garlic
1 tb. wine vinegar　peeled green chiles, cut
1 tsp. powdered red chile　into small strips

Combine the olives, oil, vinegar and spices and let stand, covered, in the refrigerator for at least 24 hours. To serve, drain and stuff with green chile, then stick each olive with a toothpick.

SPICED OYSTERS

3 doz. fresh oysters
2 tb. lemon juice
1 tb. salt
1½ cups chopped Spanish onion
½ cup olive oil
1 cup white wine vinegar
1 tsp. allspice

3 drops Tabasco sauce
2 pressed cloves of garlic
1 tsp. MSG
1 minced pickled jalapeño
pepper with 1 tsp. juice
from jar

Simmer shucked oysters with a cup of water, the lemon juice and salt. Sauté the onion in olive oil until it is transparent and add to oysters. Add the rest of the ingredients and let stand, covered, in the refrigerator for at least 24 hours. Serve with toothpicks.

CHILE CON QUESO

¼ cup minced onion
2 tb. butter
1 cup tomatoes, peeled, seeded
and chopped (or 1 cup of
chopped canned tomatoes)
1 4-oz. can of peeled green
chiles, chopped

¼ cup cream
½ lb. grated Monterey Jack
cheese
salt to taste
6 or more drops of Tabasco
sauce

Sauté the onion in butter until transparent, then add the tomatoes and chiles. Cook slowly for 15 minutes, or until all the liquid from the tomatoes is absorbed. Add the cream, and when it begins to bubble, add the cheese. Stir slowly over a very low flame until it is melted, then add salt and Tabasco sauce. Serve in a chafing dish with cocktail tostadas. Serves 6-8.

CREAM CHEESE AND
GREEN PEPPER PIE

1½ cup cheese wafers
½ cup butter
1 tsp. chili powder
8 oz. cream cheese
12 oz. sour cream
1 cup green onions, chopped
¾ cup peeled green chiles, minced
½ cup pimientos, minced
2 green peppers, grated
salt to taste

2 tb. parsley, chopped
1 tsp. grated lemon rind
½ tsp. MSG
pinch of sugar
1 tsp. dried oregano
1 drop Tabasco sauce
¼ cup chopped ripe olives (optional)
grated Parmesan cheese
paprika

Crush the cheese wafers with a rolling pin and place in a mixing bowl. Melt the butter and add to the cheese wafers with the chili powder. Press this mixture into a 9″ pie plate and bake in a 375° oven for 8-10 minutes. Cool.

While the crust is cooling whip the cream cheese (which should be at room temperature). When it is light and fluffy fold in the sour cream, then all the chopped vegetables and seasonings except the Parmesan cheese and paprika. Sprinkle the cheese over the top of the pie and dust lightly with paprika.

Cover the pie with foil or waxed paper and refrigerate for at least 6 hours, or overnight. The pie should be quite firm before serving and acquires more flavor if you have time to leave it overnight. Serves 6.

BEAN CROQUETTES

Make Bean Croquettes (see p. 73), but make them half as large. Serve hot with toothpicks and a bowl of Cold Green Chile Sauce (see p. 98) at the side. Serves 8.

ADDITIONAL APPETIZERS

There are several other dishes in other sections of the book which will make either excellent cocktail hors d'oeuvres or a first course dish. These are:

Avocado Slices Marinated in Rum	Guacamole
Green Garbanzo Salad	Seviche
Green Pepper Salad	Rooster's Bill

Also, of course, both pepitas and piñon nuts are often served with drinks in the Southwest. And for cocktails you will want to serve either Margaritas, or plain tequila. Tequila is drunk in this manner: each guest holds a wedge of lime between his thumb and forefinger, and a small mound of salt in the hollow at the base of his thumb—he then tastes a bit of salt, takes a swallow of tequila, and then squeezes the lime into his mouth.

Fish

FISH FILLETS WITH CHILE AND WINE

1 pressed clove of garlic	salt to taste
½ tsp. ground cumin	3 tb. olive oil
2 tsp. chili powder	½ tsp. dried oregano
3 tb. olive oil	2 tb. minced parsley
12 fish fillets	12 olives
1 green pepper, chopped	24 capers
2 tomatoes, peeled,	pinch of sugar
seeded and chopped	6 or more drops
1 cup red wine	Tabasco sauce

Mix the pressed garlic with cumin and chili powder until you have a paste. Heat the olive oil and fry the fish fillets in it. When the fish starts to brown, remove, and in the same pan fry the green pepper for 5 minutes. Add the garlic paste and the chopped tomatoes and cook another 5 minutes. Add the red wine and boil a few minutes more until the alcohol evaporates, then add the salt, sugar and Tabasco sauce.

Place the fish in layers in a shallow casserole with the tomato sauce, olive oil, parsley, oregano, olives and capers. The last layer should be of sauce and oil and herbs, etc. This is best if covered and kept overnight in the refrigerator before cooking, but it can be kept standing for only 4-5 hours if you prepare it in the middle of the day for dinner that evening. Shortly before serving, heat until bubbling in a 350° oven. Serves 6.

TROUT FROSTED WITH GUACAMOLE

1 tb. butter	1 tb. vinegar
1 tb. parsley, chopped	1 quart water
1 tb. onion, chopped	6 whole trout
3 peppercorns	guacamole (see p. 87)
1 whole clove	sliced, seeded ripe olives
½ bay leaf	parsley sprigs
1 tsp. salt	

Sauté the onion and parsley for a few minutes in the butter then add the spices, herbs, vinegar and water. Bring to the boiling point and simmer for 15 minutes. Poach the whole trout in this court bouillon just until the flesh is white and flakes with a fork.

Remove the fish carefully, then remove skin and bone, leaving the head intact. Chill the fish, and when you are ready to serve frost completely with the guacamole. Place a ripe olive ring for an eye, and garnish with parsley sprigs. Serves 6.

ESCABECHE OF SHRIMP

⅔ cup olive oil	pinch of black pepper
1 cup chopped onions	¼ tsp. dry mustard
3 pressed cloves of garlic	2 pickled jalapeño peppers,
2 lb. shrimp, uncooked	seeded and minced
½ cup lemon juice	1 cup green onions, chopped
1½ tsp. salt	

Sauté the onion and garlic in ⅓ cup of olive oil until the onion is transparent. Add the shrimp and cook 5 minutes more. Remove from heat and cool. Mix the other ingredients and add the shrimp. Marinate, covered, in the refrigerator for 24 hours, basting several times. Serve as a first course. Serves 4-6.

MEXICAN DEVILED CRAB

½ cup chopped onion
1 pressed clove of garlic
1 tb. olive oil
1 cup tomatoes, peeled,
  seeded and chopped
⅛ tsp. each of ground
  cloves and cinnamon
1 tb. chopped parsley
1 cup crab meat
6 chopped green olives

1 tsp. capers
1 pickled jalapeño pepper,
  seeded and minced
1 peeled green chile,
  chopped
4-6 drops Tabasco sauce
salt to taste
3 eggs, separated
2 tb. Parmesan cheese
2 tb. bread crumbs

Sauté the onion and garlic in olive oil until the onion is transparent. Then add the tomatoes, spices and chopped parsley. Cook 5 more minutes, then add the crab, olives, capers, chiles, Tabasco and salt.

Beat the whites of the eggs until stiff, then the yolks until creamy. Fold the yolks and the Parmesan cheese into the whites. Place the crab mixture in a shallow casserole, or individual shells, and spread the soufflé mixture on top. Sprinkle with bread crumbs. Bake at 350° until the top is brown. Serves 4-6.

RED SNAPPER
WITH MEXICAN SAUCE

6 large slices of red snapper
3 tb. olive oil
1 cup chopped onion
2 pressed cloves of garlic
1 small can of tomato sauce
1 tsp. chili powder

½ tsp. dried oregano
¼ tsp. ground cumin
juice of one orange
salt to taste
pinch of black pepper
1 orange, peeled and sliced

Fry the fish lightly in the oil, then remove from pan. In the same oil, sauté the onion and garlic for 5 minutes. Then add the tomato sauce, chili powder, oregano and cumin. Simmer for 15 minutes, or until sauce begins to thicken. Remove from fire and stir in the orange juice. Add salt and pepper.

Take a shallow casserole large enough to place all the slices of fish in one layer and oil it generously, then place the sautéed fish slices in it. Pour the sauce over and top each piece of fish with an orange slice. Bake for 30 minutes, uncovered, at 350°. Serves 6.

SEVICHE - *Red Snapper*

1 lb. fish fillets
1 cup lemon juice
1 cup tomatoes, peeled,
  seeded and minced
2 pickled jalapeño peppers,
  seeded and minced
¼ cup olive oil
2 tb. dry white wine
1 tsp. dried basil
½ tsp. dried oregano
2 tb. parsley, chopped

1 tb. capers
¼ tsp. ground coriander
1 tsp. MSG
pinch of sugar
pinch of black pepper
salt to taste
2 avocados, peeled, seeded
  and sliced
1 spanish onion, cut
  into rings

Place fish fillets in a glass dish and cover with the lemon juice. This should stand several hours, turning occasionally, until the fish turns white and is "cooked." Add all the other ingredients, except the avocado slices and onion rings. Marinate in the refrigerator for several hours and serve garnished with the avocado and onion. Serves 4-6.

Eggs

HUEVOS RANCHEROS

1 cup Chile Meat Sauce, or
  1 cup Cooked Green Chile
  Sauce (see p. 98)
6 eggs

6 tortillas
grated Monterey Jack cheese
avocado slices (optional)

Heat the sauce until it bubbles. In another pan, fry the eggs, then lightly fry the tortillas until they are softened—*they should not be crisp.* Place an egg on each tortilla, then some of the hot sauce. Sprinkle with grated cheese, and garnish with avocado slices if you wish. Serves 6.

WITH REFRIED BEANS

6 eggs
6 tortillas
hot fat
grated Monterey Jack Cheese

¾ cup refried beans (see p. 71)
cooked Green Chile sauce
  (see p. 98)

Fry the eggs, then lightly fry the tortillas. Spread each tortilla with hot refried beans, then top with an egg. Serve with sauce and grated cheese. Serves 6.

Note: These can also be garnished with sliced avocado.

EGGS WITH CHORIZO

½ cup crumbled chorizo
4 tortillas
8 eggs
hot fat

salt & black pepper to taste
sour cream
chopped green onions
  (optional)

Fry chorizo in a dry frying pan for 15-20 minutes. While this is fry-ing, fry the tortillas lightly and place each on a plate and keep warm in the oven. Beat the eggs and scramble them, adding salt and pepper to taste. Top each tortilla with scrambled eggs, then fried chorizo, then sour cream, then chopped green onions. Serves 4.

Note: If you wish, the onions may be omitted or replaced by Cooked Green Chile Sauce (see p. 98).

SCRAMBLED EGGS WITH TORTILLAS

3 tb. butter
4 chopped green onions
2 tomatoes, peeled, seeded
  and chopped
1 tb. minced parsley

12 tortillas
6 eggs, beaten
1 peeled green chile, chopped
salt & black pepper to taste
parmesan cheese

Melt butter in frying pan and add the onions, tomatoes and parsley. Sauté slowly for 5 minutes, then turn up heat and add the tortillas. Fry, stirring constantly, until they just begin to brown, then quickly lower heat and add the beaten eggs, green chile, salt and pepper. Keep lifting the mixture off the bottom of the pan until the eggs have set. Remove to heated plates and sprinkle with cheese. Serves 4.

Note: This makes a splendid dish for either luncheons or breakfasts. Monterey Jack cheese can be used either instead of, or in addition to, the Parmesan. For a simpler dish you may omit either the onions, tomatoes or parsley—or all three. It is good any way you make it.

GREEN CHILE AND CHEESE SOUFFLE

1 tb. butter	½ cup grated Monterey
1 tb. grated Parmesan	Jack cheese
cheese	½ cup peeled green chiles,
3 tb. butter	chopped
3 tb. flour	4 egg yolks
1 cup boiling milk	5 egg whites
½ tsp. salt	pinch of salt
2 drops Tabasco sauce	

Preheat oven to 400°. Butter a 6-cup soufflé dish and sprinkle with Parmesan cheese. Melt the 3 tb. butter in a saucepan, then stir in the flour and cook over moderate heat until the butter and flour foam together for 2 minutes without browning. Pour in the hot milk and beat with a wire whisk until blended. Add seasonings and cook on very slow heat for several minutes.

Remove from heat and add first the cheese, then chiles, then the egg yolks which have been beaten till frothy. Beat the egg whites with salt until they are stiff but not dry. Stir a spoonful of the beaten egg whites into the yolk mixture, then fold in the remainder.

Pour into soufflé dish and tap the bottom lightly on the table. Smooth the surface with the flat of a knife and then, after dipping the knife in hot water, cut a circle, 2″ deep and 2″ from the edge of the soufflé dish, into the mixture. This will make a puffed crown for the soufflé. Set on a rack in the middle of the oven and immediately turn the heat down to 375°. Do not open the oven for at least 20 minutes. In 20-30 minutes the soufflé will have puffed over the rim of the dish, and the top will be browned. Bake 4-5 minutes more to firm it a bit, then serve at once. Serves 4.

Note: This soufflé has a delicate flavor that is easily ruined by sauces, but I find that a bowl of cold Green Chile Sauce (see Sauce section) served at the side will please some guests. Swiss cheese, or half Monterey Jack and half sharp cheddar cheese, can be substituted with success in this dish.

EGGS IN SPANISH TOMATO SAUCE

1 grated green pepper
½ cup minced onion
1 pressed clove of garlic
1 tb. cooking oil
1 cup canned tomato sauce
1 tb. minced parsley

1 tsp. chili powder
salt to taste
6 eggs
1 cup grated Monterey
  Jack cheese

Grate the green pepper flesh and discard the skin. Sauté it with the onion and garlic in oil for 5 minutes. Add the tomato sauce, parsley, chili powder and salt. Cook slowly for 10 minutes more.

Place in a shallow casserole and carefully break eggs on the sauce. Salt the eggs slightly and then place the grated cheese over the whites of the eggs. The yolks should still be showing. Place in a 400° oven and bake just until the whites are firm—about 5 minutes. Serves 6.

Soups

MEXICAN MEATBALL SOUP

SOUP

1 chopped onion	1 peeled green chile,
1 tb. olive oil	chopped
1 cup canned tomatoes	¼ tsp. MSG
4 cups water	pinch of sugar
1 tsp. chili powder	salt to taste
	½ tsp. dried mint

Sauté the onion in oil until it is transparent. Sieve the tomatoes into the onion and add the water. When it comes to a boil, lower the flame and add the rest of the ingredients. Simmer the broth for 20 minutes.

MEATBALLS

½ lb. ground beef	1 pressed clove of garlic
½ lb. ground lean pork	1 peeled green chile,
¾ cup blue corn meal	chopped
(or masa harina)	¼ tsp. ground coriander
2 eggs	¼ tsp. dried oregano
1 chopped onion	1 tsp. salt

Combine all ingredients and shape into balls the size of a walnut. Drop them, one by one, into the simmering soup and cook slowly for 45 minutes more. Serves 6.

Note: The beef and the pork for these meatballs should both be as lean as possible, otherwise the soup will be very greasy.

OLD FASHIONED PINTO BEAN SOUP

4 cups cooked pinto beans   ½ cup chopped onions
   (see p. 70)   ½ cup grated sharp cheddar
½ tsp. dried oregano   cheese (or Monterey Jack)
2 peeled green chiles,

Take 4 cups of beans from the bean pot and combine them with the oregano, chiles and onions. Cook slowly for 30 minutes, adding water as necessary to keep them from burning. Put through a food mill and place back in your saucepan.

Add enough liquid from the bean pot, or water, to bring the soup to the desired consistency. It should be fairly thick. Cook a few minutes more, then place in soup plates. Add to each plate a generous sprinkling of cheese. Serve with hot tortillas. Serves 4.

BLACK BEAN SOUP with tortilla

3 tortillas   1 peeled green chile,
2 tb. olive oil   chopped
1 small onion, chopped   2 sprigs of lamb's-quarters
1 pressed clove of garlic   (or parsley)
1 can of black bean soup,   1 lemon, sliced
   with 1 can of water

Cut the tortillas into small pieces with scissors, and fry until crisp in the olive oil. Remove the tortillas from the pan and drain on absorbent paper. Sauté the onion and garlic in the oil till the onion is transparent. Add the black bean soup with water, the green chile, lamb's-quarters and ¾ of the fried tortillas. Simmer for 10 minutes. Garnish with lemon slices topped with the rest of the fried tortillas. Serves 4.

AVOCADO SOUPS

HOT

6 tb. grated Monterey Jack   2 avocados, peeled, seeded
cheese (or Swiss cheese)   and sliced
3 cups boiling beef stock

Place 1 tb. grated cheese in each soup plate and then pour the hot stock over it. Garnish with the avocado slices and serve immediately. Serves 4.

COLD, NUMBER ONE

1 cup tomato juice   pinch of sugar
½ cup chopped green onions   2 tb. lemon juice
1 clove of garlic   1 can of condensed beef
1 tsp. salt   bouillon, with enough water
1 pinch of black pepper   to make 3 cups
1 whole clove   1 avocado, peeled, seeded
½ tsp. dried basil   and sliced
½ bay leaf   4 tb. sour cream
2 drops of Tabasco sauce

Place the tomato juice in a saucepan, and add the onion, garlic, spices, Tabasco sauce, sugar and lemon juice. Boil for 10 minutes, then cool slightly, strain the broth and add the beef bouillon and water. Heat to boiling and then chill thoroughly in the refrigerator. Before serving slice avocados into soup plates, pour the soup over and add to each a spoonful of sour cream. Serves 4.

COLD, NUMBER TWO

4 cups cold chicken broth   1 tsp. salt
2 cups diced avocados   pinch of black pepper
¼ cup lime juice (or lemon)   parsley (or chives)

Place all the ingredients but the parsley in a blender and mix until smooth. Chill for an hour, covered, in the refrigerator and serve in cold soup plates garnished with a sprig of parsley or chopped chives. Serves 6.

PUREÉ OF GARBANZO SOUP

2 cups cooked garbanzos   ¼ tsp. dried oregano
(see p. 74)   salt to taste
4 cups chicken broth   2 tb. butter
2 cups water   4 drops Tabasco sauce
½ cup chopped onion   2 eggs
1 pressed clove of garlic   4 chorizos
2 tb. chopped parsley

Place the garbanzos, broth, water, onions, garlic, parsley and oregano in a saucepan and simmer for 30 minutes. Pureé in a blender, or sieve the garbanzos, until you have a soup the consistency of cream. If it is too thick you may add more chicken broth, or water. Mix in the butter and Tabasco sauce. Beat the eggs in a bowl and gradually add the hot soup, stirring constantly. Reheat, but do not let the soup boil. Slice the chorizos and fry for 10-15 minutes. Garnish the soup with the fried chorizos. Serves 6.

LYLE'S JELLED GARLIC SOUP

2 heads of garlic cloves
1 large onion, chopped
1 tb. butter
3 cans of beef consommé with
  1 can of water
1 envelope gelatine

2 slices of lime peel
½ tsp. dried mint
  (or 2 leaves of fresh)
⅛ cup lime juice
6 drops of Tabasco sauce
1 lime, sliced

Separate the cloves of garlic, peel them, and slice thinly. Sauté the garlic and onion in the butter until golden. Place the consommé in a large saucepan and bring it to a boil, then add the garlic and onion.

Put a bit of water in one of the cans and add the gelatine. Stir until the gelatine is softened and add enough water to fill the can. Add to the boiling soup, stirring so the gelatine dissolves in the hot liquid. Boil gently for several hours: the longer it cooks the richer the flavor.

After you think it has cooked long enough, measure the liquid and add enough water to make 4 cups, return to the pan and add the lime peel and the mint. Simmer for 10 minutes and remove from the fire.

Add the lime juice and Tabasco sauce, then taste the soup—you may wish to add more lime juice or Tabasco sauce, but remember that a chilled soup will have less flavor than a hot one.

Strain the soup and place in the refrigerator to jell. Before it jells skim off the fat which has come to the top and hardened. When firm, scoop out with a spoon into small soup cups and serve with a slice of lime. Serves 4-6.

Note: If you feel it necessary, add more butter, or better yet, a bit of olive oil to the garlic and onions. I have used very little fat since one must skim it off before serving anyway. Lemon may be substituted for lime, if you wish. The soup can also be served hot. In this case, do not strain it, or skim the fat off.

The hot soup makes a very good meal in itself with an egg broken into each soup plate and poached as it sits in the broth: serve this with a green salad and tortillas. Do not worry about the amount of garlic, since after cooking the garlic is mellow and rich. In fact I would suggest rather more than less garlic if you wish to change the proportion. This soup is an interesting example of a purely Spanish soup filtered through Mexico and finally adapted to American cooking methods.

MEXICAN SUMMER SOUP

¼ cup chopped green onions
2 cups sliced summer squash
  (or zucchini)
1 tb. olive oil
2 tb. tomato paste
2 cups chicken broth
1 cup cooked, diced chicken

1 cup fresh, frozen, or
  canned corn
½ tsp. dried oregano
½ tsp. chili powder
2 avocados peeled, seeded
  and cubed
1 3-oz. package cream cheese

Sauté onions and squash in olive oil for 5 minutes. Add tomato paste and cook a few minutes longer. Add broth, chicken, corn and herbs. Cook gently 15-20 minutes. Just before serving add the cubed avocados. Place in bowls and garnish with cream cheese cut into cubes. Serve with hot tortillas. Serves 6-8.

TEXAS GAZPACHO

1 can beef bouillon with
  1 can of water
1 cup chopped Spanish onion
1 grated green pepper
6 tomatoes, peeled, seeded
  and chopped
¼ cup chopped parsley
salt to taste
pinch of black pepper
1 tb. fresh basil
  (or 1 tsp. dried)

3 tb. lemon juice
  (or lime)
4 drops Tabasco sauce
pinch of sugar
½ pressed clove of garlic
1 tb. red wine
1 tsp. ground coriander
  soaked in 1 tb. hot water
1 tsp. grated lemon rind
1 cup peeled, cubed cucumber
ice cubes

Combine all ingredients (the hot water drained from the ground coriander added, the coriander discarded) except the cucumber. Let this sit, covered, in the refrigerator for at least an hour. When you are ready to serve the soup add the cucumber and place in cold soup plates. Add two ice cubes to each plate, and serve. Serves 6.

Meat

BAKED PORK LOIN
WITH ORANGES

1½ lbs. pork loin	½ cup grated onion
1 tsp. salt	1 pressed clove of garlic
¼ tsp. black pepper	1 mashed banana
1-2 pickled jalapeño peppers,	1 cup orange juice
seeded and minced	1 tb. chili powder
3 slices of bacon	sliced, peeled oranges

Remove most of the fat from the pork and melt it in a frying pan, then brown roast in the fat. Remove from the pan, salt and pepper it, then sprinkle the minced jalapeños over. Lay the bacon slices on top of the roast and tie the meat with string to hold bacon and peppers on top.

Place in a roaster and cover with a sauce made from the combined onion, garlic, banana, orange juice and chili powder. Cover the pan and cook at 350° for 1½ hours. Baste the meat with the sauce at least two times during the cooking.

When the meat is done, remove from the pan and snip the strings carefully so as not to disturb the sauce on top of the meat. Place on a platter and keep warm. If there is a great deal of fat in the pan, skim most of it off, then stir the sauce and spoon some over meat. Put the rest in a sauceboat to serve at the table. Garnish the roast with sliced, peeled oranges. Serves 6 to 8.

31

PORK CHOPS AND KIDNEY BEANS

6 pork chops
1 tsp. salt
¼ tsp. black pepper
½ cup olive oil
2 cups water
2 cups chopped onion
2 pressed cloves of garlic

½ cup peeled green chiles,
    cut into strips
4 drops Tabasco sauce
3 cups cooked kidney beans
    (see Beans & Rice Section)
1 thinly sliced onion
½ cup grated cheddar cheese

Season the chops with salt and pepper and brown in ¼ cup olive oil. Then add the water, cover and cook over low heat for 30 minutes. Sauté the onion and garlic in the other ¼ cup olive oil until the onion is transparent. Add the green chiles, Tabasco sauce and kidney beans, then add all to pork chops. Cover and cook slowly another 30 minutes. Serve with onion slices on top and grated cheese. Serves 6.

POSOLE

Make Pork Filling (see p. 52) and add 3 cups of hominy during the last 10 minutes of cooking. Serves 4.

TINGA

2 cups cooked pork
1 tb. bacon fat
½ cup chopped onion
1 pressed clove of garlic
½ cup crumbled chorizo
1 cup tomatoes, peeled,
  seeded and chopped
salt to taste
1 pickled jalapeño pepper,
  seeded and minced

½ cup stock from boiled pork,
  or thinned gravy from leftover
  pork roast
1 cup water
1 tsp. salt
1 tb. vinegar
1 onion sliced in rings
1 avocado, peeled, seeded
  and sliced

Either use leftover baked pork or boil a pork loin until very tender. Shred the meat. In a frying pan melt the bacon fat and sauté the onion and garlic in it until the onion is transparent. Add the chorizo and fry for 10 minutes longer. Then add tomatoes, salt, jalapeño, shredded pork, and stock.

Let most of the liquid cook away so the meat begins to brown slightly, then remove from fire. Soak the onion rings in water with salt and vinegar. Peel and slice the avocado and serve the Tinga garnished with onion and avocado. Serves 4.

Note: This makes a very good taco filling.

LEG OF LAMB IN CHILE & WINE SAUCE

Leg of lamb, boned
1 cup red wine
½ cup orange juice
1 tb. chili powder
¼ cup peeled green chiles, chopped
2 tb. olive oil
1 medium onion, chopped

2 pressed cloves of garlic
½ tsp. dried oregano
1 tsp. ground cumin
1 tb. brown sugar
1 bay leaf
grated rind of one orange
1 tsp. salt

Have lamb boned at market for easier cutting, remove most of fat and membrane covering meat and place in a glass dish or enamel pan. Combine all ingredients and marinate the lamb in the refrigerator for 24 hours. Turn several times during this period.

Lift meat out, drain, and place on rack in a roaster. Preheat oven to 450°, place meat in the oven for 15 minutes, then turn heat down to 350° and pour marinade around the meat.

Cook 25 minutes to the pound for pink lamb—30 minutes for well done. If the lamb has not been boned, subtract 5 minutes per pound. When ready to serve, remove meat and let sit at room temperature for 10-15 minutes. Skim off fat from the pan juices and serve in a sauce boat with the meat. Serves 6-8.

STEW WITH SQUASH BLOSSOMS

1½ lbs. stew meat—
  either lamb, veal or beef
2 quarts water
1 cup green beans, cut up
6 pieces of corn on the cob,
  cut into slices
6 squash blossoms
6 summer squash, cut up

2 tb. chopped green onions
1 pressed clove of garlic
2 tb. fresh coriander
  (or parsley)
salt to taste
pinch of sugar
3 drops Tabasco sauce

Stew meat until tender in the water, then remove from the pot and strain the stock. If it has boiled down add enough water to make 2 quarts. Add the green beans and cook until they are tender, then add the other ingredients, with meat, and cook for 30 minutes. Serves 4-6.

PICADILLO

½ lb. ground beef (or veal)
½ lb. ground pork
1 chopped onion
1 cup canned tomatoes
2 pressed cloves of garlic
1 tb. vinegar
pinch of sugar

1 tsp. cinnamon
pinch of ground cloves
¼ tsp. ground cumin
1 tsp. salt
1 bay leaf
½ cup seedless raisins
½ cup blanched, slivered almonds

Place the meats in a frying pan and when they begin to release the fat add both the onion and the garlic. When the meat browns add all the ingredients except the raisins and the almonds, and simmer for 30 minutes. Then add the raisins and almonds and simmer for another 5-10 minutes.

Note: This is a good dish as is, but is most often served as a stuffing for tacos, tamales, chicken, or best of all—green chiles. Serves 4.

MEXICAN ROUND STEAK

3 lbs. round steak	3 tb. olive oil
2 tsp. salt	2 cups chopped onion
½ tsp. powdered red chile	1 tb. chili powder
1 pressed clove of garlic	3 tomatoes, peeled and sliced
4 tb. flour	½ cup beef broth

Rub the salt, powdered chile, garlic and flour into the meat, then pound the steak (it should be all one piece). Brown the steak on both sides in the olive oil, then place in a casserole.

Sauté onions in the same fat, and when they are transparent, spread them over the steak. Cover and bake at 350° for 1 hour. Add the chili powder and tomatoes and bake for another half hour. Finally, add the beef broth and bake, uncovered, for 20 minutes, or until tender. Serves 4-6.

GRILLED STEAKS WITH GUACAMOLE

Grill, or broil, steaks and served topped with cold guacamole (see p. 87).

COLD ROAST BEEF WITH GAUCAMOLE

Slice leftover roast beef very thinly and serve spread with guacamole (see p. 87).

MEXICAN MEATLOAF

1 lb. ground round
½ cup crumbled chorizo
½ cup chopped ripe olives
½ cup chopped onion
½ cup white cornmeal
½ cup peeled green chiles,
   chopped

1 pickled jalapeño pepper,
   seeded and minced
1 tsp. chili powder
½ tsp. dried oregano
pinch of ground cumin
salt to taste
avocado slices

Combine all the ingredients except the avocado and place in a greased loaf pan. Cook at 350° for 1 hour. Serve with slices of avocado on the top of the loaf—and Cold Green Chile Sauce (see p. 98) if you wish. Serves 4.

CHILE MEATLOAF
STUFFED WITH PINTO BEANS

1½ lbs. ground round
1 cup Chile Meat sauce
   (see p. 99)
1 tsp. salt
1 cup cooked pinto beans
   (see p. 70)

⅓ cup peeled green chiles,
   chopped
¾ cup grated sharp cheddar
   cheese
⅓ cup Chile Meat Sauce
   (see p. 99)

Mix ground round with 1 cup Chile Meat Sauce and the salt. Line the bottom and sides of a loaf pan with ¾ of the mixture. Mash the pinto beans and add the green chile and cheese. Fill the pocket made in the loaf pan by the meat with this bean mixture. Then carefully top the beans with the rest of the meat so that they are completely covered and sealed in. Spread the other ⅓ cup of meat sauce over the top of the loaf and place in a 350° oven. Bake for 1 hour. Serves 4.

CHORIZO

1 lb. lean pork, ground	¼ tsp. black pepper
1 tsp. salt	pinch of ginger
1½-2 tb. powdered red chile	pinch of nutmeg
¼ tsp. ground cloves	pinch of ground coriander
¼ tsp. cinnamon	1 crumbled bay leaf
¼ tsp. dried oregano	4 pressed cloves of garlic
¼ tsp. dried thyme	1 tb. vinegar
¼ tsp. ground cumin	sausage casings (optional)

If you have the pork ground at the market have them grind it twice since it should not be too coarse. Mix all the ingredients thoroughly and let it stand covered in the refrigerator for 24 hours.

This mixture can then be stuffed into sausage casings if you wish or can be kept in a jar in the refrigerator. This will keep for a couple of weeks or more.

To cook, fry the sausage either crumbled, or in patties, or as sausages if you have stuffed them. They will need no extra fat and will be done in 15-20 minutes over a medium flame.

CHILE CON CARNE

Add to Chile Meat Sauce (see p. 99) the desired amount of either cooked pinto, or kidney beans.

CHILAQUILES

8 tortillas
hot fat
¾ cup crumbled chorizo
½ cup minced onion
1 pressed clove of garlic
½ cup tomato sauce
½ pickled jalapeño pepper,
 seeded and chopped
¼ tsp. ground red chile

pinch of sugar
½ tsp. MSG
1½ cups Monterey Jack
 cheese, grated
¼ cup Parmesan cheese
½ cup ripe olives (optional)
1 avocado, peeled, seeded
 and sliced
1 small onion cut into rings

Cut the tortillas into small strips with scissors and fry in hot fat, just until soft. Remove with a slotted spoon and drain on absorbent paper.

Pour the oil out of the pan, place it back on the fire and fry the chorizo until it begins to crisp. Remove from the pan and add minced onion and the garlic. When the onion is transparent, add the tomato sauce, the jalapeño, ground chile, sugar and MSG.

Cook until the sauce thickens and remove from fire. Place a layer of tortillas in the bottom of a casserole, then some chorizo, then tomato sauce, then ripe olives if used, then Monterey Jack, then Parmesan. Repeat the layers and place the casserole in a 350° oven for about 20 minutes. Serve with sliced avocado and onion rings on top. Serves 4.

Poultry

FRIED CHICKEN
WITH COLD GREEN CHILE SAUCE

2 small chickens cut
  for frying
3 tb. parsley, minced
¼ tsp. dried thyme
1 tsp. chili powder
1 pressed clove of garlic
½ tsp. MSG
juice of one lemon
1 tsp. salt
1 egg

½ cup water
½ cup milk
1½ cups sifted flour
½ tsp. salt
1 tsp. baking soda
1 tsp. dried thyme
hot fat
Cold Green Chile Sauce
  (see p. 98)

Combine 2 tb. parsley, thyme, chili powder, garlic, MSG, lemon juice and salt. Marinate chicken in this for 2 or more hours. Then drain chicken and dip in the following batter: combine egg, water, milk, flour, salt, soda, thyme and 1 tb. parsley. Drop the chicken into hot fat and cook until it is deep golden brown. Drain on absorbent paper and serve with Cold Green Chile Sauce. Serves 4-6.

CHICKEN
WITH PUMPKINSEED SAUCE

1 chicken, cut up	pinch of black pepper
2 carrots, peeled and sliced	½ cup pepitas
	¼ cup blanched almonds
1 sliced onion	3 peeled green chiles
1 tb. parsley	⅓ cup parsley
1 bay leaf	2 cups chicken broth
2 whole cloves	1 tb. lemon juice
1 tsp. dried oregano	pinch of sugar
1 tsp. dried basil	¼ tsp. MSG
salt to taste	1 tb. butter

Boil the chicken until tender with vegetables, spices and herbs. Strain broth and place in the refrigerator until the fat hardens, then remove fat and measure 2 cups of broth.

To make sauce, place the pepitas, almonds, chiles, parsley and some of the broth in the blender and mix until smooth. Place in a saucepan and cook 20-30 minutes, or until it begins to thicken. Add lemon juice, sugar, MSG and butter and cook a few minutes longer. Place the chicken in a casserole and pour sauce over, cover, and cook in a 350° oven for 30 minutes. Serves 4.

Note: This sauce is also good to cook fish fillets in, and it can be used well with leftover turkey.

CHICKEN

CASSEROLE WITH GREEN CHILES

1 chicken, cut up
½ cup flour
1 tsp. salt
1 tsp. chili powder
hot fat
4 strips bacon, minced
3 sliced carrots
1 small chopped onion

1 can peeled green chiles,
  chopped
1 tb. minced parsley
1 bay leaf
⅛ tsp. dried thyme
1 sliced lemon
2 cups tomato juice

Shake the chicken in a bag with flour, salt and chili powder. Fry in hot fat until golden. Remove to a casserole and add the rest of the ingredients except the lemon and tomato juice. Lay the lemon slices on top of the chicken pieces and pour the tomato juice over. Bake at 350°, covered, for 1 hour. Serves 4.

WITH GREEN CHILES AND SOUR CREAM

2 cups chopped onion
1 can peeled green chiles,
  chopped
2 tb. butter
2 cups diced cooked chicken

1 cup sour cream
salt to taste
1 cup Monterey Jack cheese,
  grated (or ¼ cup grated
  Parmesan cheese)

Sauté the onion and green chiles in the butter until the onion is transparent. Then add the chicken and when it is heated through add the sour cream and salt. Do not let it boil. Serve hot with grated cheese on top and with hot tortillas. Serves 4.

CHICKEN (OR TURKEY) MOLE

1 chicken or turkey cut
  into serving pieces
water
1 onion
1 clove of garlic
salt to taste

1 bay leaf
¼ cup oil
¼ cup butter
Mole Sauce (see p. 100)
toasted sesame seeds

Boil chicken or turkey until just tender in the water with onion, garlic, salt and bay leaf. Double amounts for turkey. Sauté the fowl in oil and butter until it begins to brown, then place in a casserole and cover with Mole Sauce. Cook at 350° for 30 minutes. Serve sprinkled with sesame seeds which have been placed in a dry frying pan and shaken over a low flame until they are golden. Serves 4-12.

Note: This gains in flavor by being reheated the second day.

TURKEY WITH GARBANZO STUFFING

Stuff your turkey with Puree of Garbanzos (see p. 74). Then roast in your favorite manner. At serving time remove the stuffing from the turkey and place in a serving dish. Pour some of the juices from the pan over the top then sprinkle with toasted and salted piñon nuts. Serves 8-12.

Barbecues

SPARERIBS

5 lbs. spareribs	2 pressed cloves of garlic
salt	½ cup white wine
pepper	juice of one lemon
paprika	pinch of sugar

Cut spareribs into serving pieces and rub with salt, pepper and paprika. Place in a glass or enamel dish. Combine all the other ingredients and pour over ribs. Marinate overnight.

SAUCE

1 cup chopped onion	½ tsp. ground cumin
¼ cup diced celery	2 tb. Worcestershire sauce
bacon fat	2 tb. brown sugar
½ cup canned tomatoes	2 tb. chili powder
½ cup tomato sauce	2 pickled jalapeño peppers,
1 tb. prepared mustard	seeded and minced
1 tsp. dried thyme	1 cup vinegar

Mix all ingredients and boil for 2 minutes. Drain the ribs from the marinade and brush each with some of the sauce. Broil over charcoal until they are very brown, turning and basting every 15 minutes. Serves 6.

PORK CHOPS

3 tb. chili powder	1 tsp. salt
3 tb. tomato juice	⅛ tsp. dried oregano
4 pressed cloves of garlic	8 pork chops

Combine all the ingredients to make a paste and spread on the chops. Marinate overnight, then grill over charcoal.

Note: These are also good first browned in a frying pan, then baked in a medium oven, with a bit of water added to them, for 45 minutes. Serve with Cold Green Chile Sauce (see p. 98). Serves 4.

VEAL (OR LAMB) CHOPS

½ tsp. dried thyme	⅓ cup red wine
½ tsp. ground cumin	¼ cup olive oil
½ tsp. dried oregano	½ cup tomato sauce
1 tb. chili powder	1 pressed clove of garlic
1 tsp. salt	1 tsp. lime juice (or lemon)
1 cup chopped onion	6 chops about 1½" thick

Combine ingredients and marinate chops at least 4 hours. Cook over charcoal while you baste with the marinade. Serves 3.

STEAKS

1 pressed clove of garlic	2 tsp. wine vinegar
2 tb. chili powder	1 tsp. MSG
¼ tsp. dried oregano	steaks

Combine herbs and vinegar and MSG to make a paste. Rub this into the steaks and let them stand for 3-4 hours. Grill over charcoal. Salt steak as you serve it.

WITH JALAPEÑO SAUCE

Grill steaks (or hamburgers) over charcoal and serve with Jalapeño Sauce (see p. 101).

HAMBURGERS

WITH CHILE MEAT SAUCE

Grill hamburgers and top with Chile Meat Sauce (see p. 99). Serve with bowls of chopped onion, grated cheese, chopped lettuce and Cold Green Chile Sauce (see p. 98).

WITH GUACAMOLE

Combine hamburger with salt, pepper and chopped, peeled green chiles. Grill over charcoal and serve topped with Guacamole (see p. 87).

CHICKEN

1 cup red wine
½ cup orange juice
1 tb. chili powder
¼ cup peeled green chiles,
  chopped
2 tb. olive oil
1 onion, chopped
2 pressed cloves of garlic

½ tsp. dried oregano
1 tsp. ground cumin
1 tb. brown sugar
1 bay leaf
grated rind of one orange
salt to taste
1 chicken whole, or cut up

Combine marinade and let chicken stand in it overnight in the refrigerator. You can either spit-roast a whole chicken or grill chicken parts over charcoal, basting with the marinade. Serves 4.

Note: This sauce is also excellent with lamb chops.

SHRIMP

½ cup butter
1 tb. lemon juice
1½ tsp. chili powder
½ tsp. salt

⅛ tsp. dried oregano
pinch of black pepper
1 lb. shrimp

Combine all ingredients except the shrimp. Place shrimp on skewers and brush with sauce as you cook over charcoal. Serves 2-4.

Tamale Pies

CHICKEN-CHEESE TAMALE PIE

FILLING

1 chicken
3 large onions
2 cloves of garlic
1 bay leaf
1 tsp. dried basil
2 whole cloves
3 peppercorns
½ tsp. salt
2 peeled green chiles, chopped

1 pickled jalapeño pepper, seeded and minced
1 cup chopped ripe olives
1 tsp. MSG
pinch of sugar
1 tsp. chili powder
2 cups sour cream
2 cups Monterey Jack cheese, grated

Boil the chicken with onions, garlic and next 5 ingredients. Remove meat from bones and reserve 2 cups of chicken. Dice the chicken. Drain broth from the vegetables and reserve 2 cups for the topping. Combine the chicken, the onions it was cooked with, chopped, and all the other ingredients except the cheese and place in the bottom of a casserole. Top with the grated cheese and then the following mixture:

48

TAMALE MIXTURE

2 cups chicken broth   ½ cup Monterey Jack cheese,
1 cup masa harina   grated
2 eggs, separated   whole ripe olives

Bring the broth to a boil and add the masa gradually, beating constantly. Cook for 5-10 minutes while it thickens, over a very slow fire,
stirring to prevent burning. Remove from the fire and add the egg
yolks. Whip the whites till stiff and fold them into the mush. Spread
this over the filling in the casserole and sprinkle with cheese and
decorate with olives. Bake at 375° for 30-40 minutes. Serves 4.

TAMALE MIXTURES

NUMBER ONE

2 cups masa harina
1⅓ cups warm water
1 cup whipping cream
¼ cup butter

4 eggs, separated
1 tsp. salt
1 tsp. baking powder
¼ cup Parmesan cheese

Blend the masa with warm water, then with cream. Melt butter and add to the masa, beating in thoroughly. Add egg yolks, one by one, still beating, then salt and baking powder. Beat egg whites till stiff, but not dry, and fold into masa mixture. Place half in bottom of a 2 quart casserole, then add a filling, (pp. 51-52) then top with the rest of the tamale mixture. Bake for 45 minutes at 350° then sprinkle with Parmesan cheese and cook 15 more minutes.

NUMBER TWO

1½ cups milk
1 tsp. salt
2 tb. butter

½ cup corn meal
1 cup Monterey Jack cheese, grated
2 beaten eggs

Heat milk almost to boiling, then add salt and butter. Stir the corn meal into the milk slowly, beating constantly to prevent lumps. Simmer for 15 minues making sure the mixture doesn't burn on the bottom. Line both sides and bottom of a casserole with the mush and pour a filling (pp. 51-52) in. Cover with the rest of the mush. Bake at 350° for 1 hour.

NUMBER THREE

2 cups masa harina
(or blue cornmeal)

2 tsp. salt
6 cups boiling water (or beef stock)

Stir masa slowly into boiling salted water, or beef stock. Simmer for 15 minutes, stirring the mush to keep it from burning. Line both sides and bottom of a casserole with the mush and pour a filling (see pp. 51-52) in. Cover with the rest of the mush. Bake at 350° for 1 hour.

FILLINGS

CHICKEN

2 tb. butter	12 stuffed green olives, chopped
½ cup grated onion	½ cup raisins
2 cup grated onion	¼ cup ground almonds
4 peeled green chiles, chopped	salt to taste
2 cups cooked chicken, diced	

Sauté onion in butter until it becomes transparent, then add tomatoes and cook a few minutes more. Add the rest of the ingredients but be sure to taste for salt as the olives are salty. Cook for 5-10 minutes slowly.

BEEF

¼ cup olive oil	1 tsp. salt
1 cup chopped onion	2 tb. chili powder
½ cup grated green pepper	pinch of black pepper
1 pressed clove of garlic	½ cup corn meal
1½ lbs. ground beef	1 cup water
2½ cups canned tomatoes	1 cup chopped ripe olives

Sauté the onions and garlic and green pepper in olive oil for 5 minutes, then remove from pan. Sauté beef, and when it begins to brown add the onions, tomatoes, salt, pepper and chili powder. Simmer for 10 minutes. Stir the corn meal into the water and add to the meat mixture. Cook slowly for 10 more minutes. Add olives.

PORK FILLING

2 lbs. pork	1 cup canned tomatoes
½ cup water	1 can peeled green chiles,
2 cloves of garlic	chopped
¼ tsp. black pepper	1 tsp. ground coriander
½ tsp. salt	soaked in 1 tb. of
½ cup chopped onion	hot water

Remove most of fat from pork and cut into cubes. Cook meat with water, garlic, salt and pepper until all the water is absorbed, then discard the garlic and let the meat brown in its own fat.

Add the onion and cook 5 more minutes, slowly. Add tomatoes, chiles and the water drained from the coriander. Taste for salt and add more if needed. Cook, covered, for 30 minutes.

Note: This makes a good dish by itself with 1 cup of canned corn added, or three ears of corn cut into 1" pieces. Also it makes the best posole with 3 cups of hominy added. Either corn or hominy should be added the last 10 minutes of cooking.

Dishes Using Tortillas

CHEESE ENCHILADAS

WITH MEAT SAUCE

Fry tortillas lightly—just until they soften. Drain on absorbent paper. Heat Chile Meat Sauce (see p. 98) and dip the tortillas into the sauce, then place on a warm plate. Sprinkle each tortilla with 1 tablespoon grated cheese and 1 tablespoon minced green onion. Roll up, sprinkle cheese on the top and heat in a medium oven till the cheese melts. Serve with extra meat sauce.

Note: Either Spanish onion or green onion is best in these enchiladas (see Ingredients & Methods to treat regular onion to make it milder). The cheese may be varied in any way you wish, though I do not recommend processed American cheese. Monterey Jack cheese, or a sharp cheddar, or a combination of both, is most often used in the Southwest. But especially delicious are either Greek Feta cheese or the Italian Provolone: these are closer to the goat cheese used in Mexico. Also chopped ripe olives give an added flavor, either included in the filling or as a garnish.

WITH RED CHILE SAUCE

Make enchiladas as above, but substitute Red Chile Sauce (see p. 97) for Chile Meat Sauce.

ENCHILADAS

WITH GREEN CHILE SAUCE

12 tortillas
hot fat
½ cup chopped green onion
1 pressed clove of garlic
1 tb. chopped parsley
1 green pepper, grated
1 tb. olive oil
1 can of tomatillo,
  drained and sieved

1 can peeled green chiles,
  chopped
salt to taste
pinch of sugar
pinch of ground coriander
1 cup milk
1 tb. cornstarch
1¾ cup Monterey Jack
  cheese, grated

Fry tortillas lightly in the fat and drain on absorbent paper. Sauté onion, garlic, parsley and green pepper in the oil for 5 minutes. Add the tomatillo, the green chiles and cook several minutes more. Add salt, sugar and coriander. Dissolve cornstarch in the milk and add to the pan. Cook slowly for 10 minutes.

Remove from the heat and add 1 cup of grated cheese. Place a tortilla on a warm plate, top with some of the sauce, then add another tortilla, topping each layer, in turn, with sauce. You may make either four stacks of three or three stacks of four in this way. There should be more sauce over the final tortilla than between the layers. To serve, sprinkle with the rest of the grated cheese. Serves 4.

WITH SOUR CREAM

Fry tortillas lightly, sprinkle each with Parmesan cheese, and place a dollop of sour cream on each, then spoon some cooked Green Chile Sauce (see p. 97) on it. Roll up and place in a shallow casserole. Bake in a medium oven for 5-10 minutes. Serve with sauce spooned over the top and a bit more sour cream.

CREAM CHEESE ENCHILADAS

2 tb. chopped green onion
1 green pepper, grated
2 tb. olive oil
¼ cup canned tomatoes, chopped
along with ¼ cup of the
juice from the can

1 3-oz. package cream cheese
6 tortillas
1 cup Monterey Jack cheese,
grated
salt to taste
chili powder

Sauté the onion and green pepper in the oil for 5 minutes. Add the tomatoes with their juice and simmer 10 minutes more, or until the sauce thickens slightly and the juice is absorbed. Add the cream cheese and stir till it is melted. Fry tortillas lightly and drain on absorbent paper. Sprinkle lightly with salt and chili powder. Divide the cream cheese mixture among the tortillas and roll them. Place in a shallow baking dish and sprinkle with cheese. Place in a 350° oven till the cheese melts and serve. Serves 3.

AVOCADO ENCHILADAS

tortillas
hot fat

Guacamole (see p. 87)
cooked Green Chile Sauce
(see p. 97)

Fry the tortillas lightly in hot fat then drain on absorbent paper. Fill the warm tortillas with guacamole and roll up. Serve with the chile sauce.

BEAN ENCHILADAS

NUMBER ONE

tortillas	chopped green onion
bacon fat	grated sharp cheddar cheese
pinto beans (see p. 70)	chili powder
pickled jalapeño peppers,	salt
seeded and minced	

Fry tortillas lightly in a small amount of bacon fat until they just puff up. Drain on absorbent paper. Heat pinto beans and fill the tortillas with 3-4 tb. of beans taken out of the bean pot with a slotted spoon. Add a sprinkling of jalapeño, onions and cheese. Roll up, spoon some of the bean liquid over each, and dust with salt and chili powder. Serve immediately.

Note: These are best made with pinto beans cooked from the dried beans rather than with the canned variety. The bacon fat, here, gives a better flavor to the enchilada, especially if the beans are being reheated.

NUMBER TWO

12 tortillas	2-3 pickled jalapeño peppers,
hot fat	seeded and minced
2 cups cooked pinto beans	1 cup cream
1 tsp. salt	chopped green onion

Fry tortillas lightly and drain on absorbent paper. Mix beans with jalapeños and place in layers in a casserole with tortillas, ending with a tortilla. Mix salt into cream and pour over the tortillas and beans. Bake, uncovered, at 350° till all the cream is absorbed and the dish is bubbling. Serve sliced into pie-shaped wedges sprinkled with chopped green onion. Serves 4-6.

PORK ENCHILADAS

9 tortillas
hot fat
1 cup shredded roast pork
¼ cup crumbled chorizo
½ cup chopped onion
2 tb. chopped parsley
½ pickled jalapeño pepper,
  seeded and minced
½ cup Monterey Jack cheese,
  grated

½ green pepper, grated
½ cup onion, grated
1 tsp. chili powder
pinch each of ground coriander,
  nutmeg, cloves, cinnamon,
  thyme and black pepper
salt to taste
½ cup Monterey Jack cheese,
  grated
green olives

Fry the tortillas lightly and drain on absorbent paper. To make filling, first shred the cooked pork. Then slowly fry the chorizo with chopped onion for 10 minutes. Add the pork, parsley and the jalapeño. Cook several minutes more. If the chorizo does not give enough fat add a bit extra pork or bacon fat.

Remove from the pan and add ½ cup of cheese to the meat mixture. In the fat left in the pan, or more if you need it, fry the grated green pepper and onion till the onion is transparent, then add the spices and cook a few minutes more.

Roll some of the pork mixture in each tortilla and place them in a shallow casserole. Spread the onion-pepper mixture over, then sprinkle with cheese and decorate with green olives. Bake at 350° until the enchiladas are warmed through and the cheese bubbles. Serves 3.

CHICKEN MOLE ENCHILADAS

1 small chopped onion
1 tb. oil
1 tomato, peeled, seeded and
chopped
¼ cup blanched almonds
1 tb. raisins

6 green olives
1 cup cooked, diced chicken
6 tortillas
hot fat
Mole Sauce (see p. 100)

Sauté onion in oil until it is transparent. Add the tomato and simmer for 5 minutes. Chop the almonds, raisins and olives finely and add to the tomato-onion mixture. Simmer 3 more minutes, then add the chicken and keep warm.

Fry the tortillas lightly. Drain on absorbent paper. Divide the filling equally among the tortillas which have been dipped first in the mole sauce. Roll the enchiladas and place in a shallow casserole. Heat at 350° until they are warmed through. Serve with hot mole sauce. Serves 3.

Note: These can also be sprinkled with toasted sesame seeds and garnished with radishes.

BANANA MOLE ENCHILADAS

Cut 4 bananas lengthwise, then in half. Fry lightly in butter. Dip each tortilla, after frying lightly, in hot mole sauce, then roll two pieces of banana in each. Place in a 350° oven for a few minutes, then serve with more mole sauce. Serves 4.

Note: These may sound strange, but are an excellent accompaniment to meat dishes.

AZTEC PIE

6 tortillas

2 3-oz. packages of
cream cheese

1 can peeled green chiles,
chopped

⅔ cup cream

1 tsp. salt

Spread 4 tortillas with cream cheese and sprinkle each with green chiles. Place them in a round casserole the size of a tortilla. Place the remaining two tortillas over the top. Add the salt to the cream and pour it over the tortillas. Bake, uncovered, at 350° for 20-30 minutes, or until all the cream is absorbed. Remove the two top tortillas. Serve cut into pie-shaped wedges. Serves 4.

Note: Milk can be used rather than cream if you wish.

CHICKEN & GREEN CHILE PIE

Make chicken mixture as in Chicken With Green Chiles And Sour Cream (see p. 42). Fry 6 tortillas until soft, remove from fat and drain on absorbent paper. Place the chicken in layers on the tortillas, in a casserole, and sprinkle each layer with grated Monterey Jack cheese. The last layer should be a tortilla and cheese. Bake, uncovered, at 350° for 30 minutes. Serves 4.

CHICKEN CREPES

WITH GREEN CHILE SAUCE, EMMANUEL

CREPES

¼ cup sifted flour	⅔ cup milk
½ tsp. salt	1 tb. melted butter
2 beaten eggs	

Sift flour with salt, then combine the other ingredients and add to the flour, beating until smooth with an egg beater. Or you may simply add all the ingredients to your blender and mix until smooth—scraping down any bits of flour that cling to the sides. Pour 3-4 tbs. of the mixture into a slightly greased, small frying pan. Tilt the pan to spread the batter out: these should be about 7″ in circumference. When they are lightly browned on one side, turn them and fry for a few seconds on the other side, remove and set aside.

FILLING

¼ cup grated onion	⅔ cup diced, cooked
2 tb. butter	chicken
2 tomatoes, peeled,	1 tb. raisins, chopped
seeded and chopped	1 tb. capers
½ cup ground almonds	10-12 green olives, chopped

Sauté onion in the butter for 5 minutes. Add the tomatoes and simmer for a few minutes, then add the other ingredients. Cook a few more minutes, then remove from fire. Place about 1 tb. of this mixture on each crepe, roll up and place in a shallow casserole which has been buttered. Cover with this sauce:

SAUCE

1 green pepper, grated
2 tb. butter
2 tb. grated onion
1½ cup milk
1½ tb. cornstarch

3 peeled green chiles, minced
½ cup Monterey Jack cheese, grated
salt to taste

Sauté the green pepper and onion in the butter for several minutes. Then add milk in which the cornstarch has been dissolved. Simmer slowly until the mixture thickens. Add chiles, half of the cheese, and salt. Pour over crepes and sprinkle with the rest of the cheese. Bake at 400° until the sauce begins to bubble and the crepes are slightly brown on top. Serves 4-6.

BURROS

Heat flour tortillas in a very hot oven, or under the broiler, for a few minutes—or until they begin to puff slightly. Quickly roll the filling in by placing it on one edge, rolling it once towards the middle, folding over the side edges to make an envelope, then rolling it once again. Serve with Cold Green Chile Sauce (see p. 98).

FILLING

Cooked pinto beans (see p. 70) and minced and seed pickled jalapeño peppers.

Cooked pinto beans, chopped green onion and grated cheese.

Cooked pinto beans and Chile Meat Sauce (see p. 98).

CHIMICHANGAS

Fry a burro in deep fat after it is rolled. It changes the flavor entirely and is well worth trying. If you wish a sauce serve either Cold Green Chile Sauce (see p. 98) or Jalapeño Sauce (see p. 101).

TOSTADAS

Tortillas	chopped green onions
hot fat	chopped tomatoes
pinto or kidney beans	pickled jalapeño peppers,
(see p. 70)	seeded and minced
Chile Meat Sauce (see	(or Jalapeño Sauce)
p. 99)	grated cheese
chopped lettuce	radishes (optional)

Fry tortillas in hot fat until they are crisp and golden. Keep warm in the oven until you are ready to serve the tostadas. Bring them to the table along with the other ingredients in bowls and let each guest make his own tostada. He should start first with a warm crisp tortilla, then place on it hot beans, then hot meat sauce, lettuce, onions, tomatoes, Jalapeño Sauce, grated cheese, and finally radishes. These are not, of course, eaten gracefully—but with gusto!

CYNTHIA'S WITH SOUR CREAM

12 tortillas	1 pint sour cream
hot fat	1 can peeled green chiles,
2 cups refried beans (see p. 71)	chopped
½ can undiluted black bean soup	¼ cup grated Parmesan cheese

Fry tortillas in hot fat till they are golden and crisp. Drain on absorbent paper and keep warm in the oven. Mix the refried beans with the black bean soup as the beans are frying. Mix the sour cream and green chiles together. To serve, spread the bean mixture on the warm tortillas, then top with the sour cream and chiles. Sprinkle with Parmesan cheese and serve. Serves 6.

CHORIZO TOSTADAS

6 tortillas	2 tb. olive oil
hot fat	1 3-oz. package cream cheese
½ cup crumbled chorizo	chopped lettuce
2 canned tomatoes, chopped	salt
with some of the juice from	vinegar
the can	6 chopped green onions
2-3 peeled green chiles, chopped	

Fry tortillas till crisp and drain on absorbent paper. Keep warm in the oven. Fry the chorizo in a frying pan till it begins to crisp, then also drain on absorbent paper.

Fry tomatoes with chiles in olive oil for 5 minutes, then add the cream cheese and cook slowly till it is melted, stirring constantly. Place shredded lettuce on tortillas, then some of the chorizo and sprinkle with salt and vinegar.

Then spoon some of the tomato-chile sauce over and top with chopped green onion. If the tomato-chile sauce is too thick you may add some of the canned tomato juice to make it the consistency of thick cream (it should not be so thin it drips off the tostada). Serves 3.

WITH REFRIED BEANS AND CHORIZO

Make refried beans (see Bean & Rice Section), and while they cook, sauté crumbled chorizo until it is crisp. Add chorizo to the beans with Tabasco sauce to taste. Keep warm. Chop lettuce and dress with oil, vinegar and salt. Grate Monterey Jack cheese. To serve: spread warm bean mixture on crisp fried tortillas, then lettuce, then cheese. Accompany with a bowl of Cold Green Chile Sauce (see p. 98).

AVOCADO TOSTADAS

8 tortillas
hot fat
4 avocados, peeled and
 seeded
2 tb. chopped green onion
2 tb. lemon juice

salt to taste
chopped lettuce
Cold Green Chile Sauce
 (see p. 98)
Monterey Jack cheese, grated

Fry tortillas in hot fat until they are gold and crisp. Drain on absorbent paper and keep warm in the oven. Mash avocados with salt and lemon juice, then add the chopped onions. Spread this mixture on the warm tostadas, add chopped lettuce, sauce and grated cheese. Serves 4.

SQUASH FLOWER TOSTADAS

4 tortillas
hot fat
20 squash flowers
2 cloves of garlic
2 tb. olive oil

½ cup chopped onion
¼ tsp. black pepper
salt to taste
4 tb. cream cheese

Fry tortillas until crisp in hot fat, then drain on absorbent paper and keep warm in the oven. Flatten the squash flowers with a large knife. Place the garlic in olive oil and sauté it until brown, then remove from pan.

Sauté the flowers about 3-4 minutes, then add the onion, salt and pepper, and cook until the onion is transparent. Spread the cream cheese on the warm tortillas and then top with squash flowers. Serves 4.

CHEESE TOSTADAS
WITH FLOUR TORTILLAS

NUMBER ONE

Place flour tortillas under a medium broiler flame. When they begin to puff up a bit, brush with butter and as they start to brown sprinkle with grated sharp cheddar cheese. Serve quickly when the cheese is melted, with Cold Green Chile Sauce (see p. 98).

NUMBER TWO

Proceed as above, but cover the tortilla first with Chile Meat Sauce (see p. 99), then chopped green onion, then grated Monterey Jack cheese. Serve with Jalapeño Sauce (see p. 101).

TACOS

tortillas

hot fat

Chile Meat Sauce (see p. 99)

pinto or kidney beans (see p. 70)

chopped lettuce

chopped tomatoes

chopped green onions

grated cheese

Cold Green Chile Sauce

(see p. 98)

Fry tortillas in hot fat as for tostadas, but as you are cooking them grasp them on one side with tongs while they are still pliable and fold one half over the other—not too tightly as there should be an opening of about 2″ between the two halves at the top. Turn as the tortillas fry to make sure they are crisp on both sides.

Remove from the pan and drain on absorbent paper. Keep warm in the oven until you are ready to make the tacos. Stuff the warm shells first with meat sauce, then beans, chopped lettuce, tomatoes, onions and grated cheese. Serve with a bowl of Cold Green Chile Sauce for guests to spoon over the tacos.

WITH TINGA

Make Tinga (see p. 33) and fill warm taco shells. Top with chopped avocado and onion.

CHICKEN TACOS
WITH TOMATILLO SAUCE
SAUCE

2 tb. chopped onion
1 pressed clove of garlic
1 tb. olive oil
1 cup canned tomatillo, sieved
2 peeled green chiles, chopped

pinch of sugar
¼ tsp. ground coriander
¼ tsp. MSG
4 drops Tabasco sauce
salt to taste

Sauté onion and garlic in the oil until the onion is transparent. Add the sieved tomatillo, chiles and the other ingredients and simmer for 15 minutes, then remove from stove.

FILLING

1 3-oz. package of cream cheese
¼ cup chopped onion
¼ tsp. MSG
1 tb. lemon juice
pinch of dried oregano

1 cup diced, cooked chicken
salt to taste
2 avocados, peeled, seeded
  and chopped
6 tortillas

Cream the cheese, which should be at room temperature, and add all other ingredients except the avocados and tortillas. Fry tortillas as for tacos and keep in a warm oven. Fill first with the chicken filling, then some chopped avocado, then the tomatillo sauce. Serves 3.

QUESADILLAS

Place a slice of Monterey Jack cheese on a tortilla and sprinkle with chili powder. Fold the tortilla over and fasten the edges with toothpicks. Either bake on a greased cookie sheet in a 350° oven until crisp, or fry in deep fat.

Note: If tortillas are not soft it is best to heat them before fastening with toothpicks.

WITH GREEN CHILE & GUACAMOLE

Fill each tortilla with Monterey Jack cheese, or sharp cheddar, and 2 tb. Cooked Green Chile Sauce (see p. 98). Fold over and fasten with toothpicks. Fry in deep fat and serve covered with guacamole (see p. 87).

WITH PICADILLO

Fill each tortilla with Picadillo (see p. 35), then fold over and fasten with toothpicks. Fry in deep fat and serve with Cold Green Chile Sauce (see p. 98).

WITH SQUASH FLOWERS

Fill each tortilla with finely chopped squash flowers, chopped green chile and grated cheese. Fold over, fasten with toothpicks and fry in deep fat.

Beans & Rice

PINTO OR KIDNEY BEANS

Soak 1 lb. of dried beans in water overnight. In the morning, drain the beans and discard any that look bad. Place in a large cooking pot and add plenty of cold water. Bring to a boil and add 1 onion, 1 clove of garlic, 3 slices of bacon and 2 tsp. chili powder. Simmer all day, adding hot water as it is needed to keep the beans moist. (Cold water added to the beans tends to keep them hard no matter how long they are cooked, as does adding salt at the beginning of cooking.) After the first three hours of cooking, salt to taste may be added.

When the beans are done they will be darkened to a nut brown color and there should be enough liquid left with them to cover them by about an inch. This liquid is particularly important in obtaining the right consistency when making refried beans, etc. The beans keep well in the refrigerator, and you can warm them up when needed with a little bacon fat.

Note: To use canned beans, cook for at least a half hour with some onion, garlic, chili powder and bacon fat.

FRIED, & REFRIED BEANS

Heat 4 tb. bacon fat in a frying pan. Drain 2 cups of cooked pinto beans, or kidney beans, and add them to the hot fat, mashing them as they cook with a potato masher. Cook slowly till all of the fat is absorbed, being careful not to burn.

Do not let the beans get too dry—add bean liquid from the pot as needed.

Serve as is, or topped with chopped green onions and/or grated cheese, and with Cold Green Chile Sauce (see p. 98).

To "refry" beans, heat more bacon fat in the frying pan and add mashed beans to it. Cook slowly until there is a brown crust on the bottom then turn beans over in sections to brown on the other side. Serve as above. Serves 4-6.

VARIATIONS

Top with sour cream and strips of peeled green chiles.

Add grated Monterey Jack cheese as the beans are being fried, cooking until the cheese melts into the beans.

Add pork cracklings to beans as they fry.

Fry crumbled chorizo, and when it begins to get crisp, add it to the refried beans.

Sauté ½ cup of onion in bacon fat until it is transparent, then add ½ cup tomato sauce and 1 tb. chili powder. Add mashed beans and proceed as for refried beans.

BEANS WITH BACON

4 cups cooked kidney beans
(canned will do)
6 slices diced bacon
¼ cup crumbled chorizo
6 drops Tabasco sauce
½ tsp. MSG

1 cup Monterey Jack cheese,
grated
Cocktail Tostadas (see p. 9)
Cold Green Chile Sauce
(see p. 98)

Bring beans to a boil. Fry bacon crisp and add to the beans, then mash the beans with a potato masher. Fry the chorizo until it is crisp and add to the beans, then place the mixture in the fat from the bacon and cook it, adding the Tabasco sauce and MSG, for 15 minutes. Add more liquid from the bean pot if it gets too dry. It should be quite moist, but not soupy. Place in individual ramekins and top with the grated cheese. Place in a hot oven, or under the broiler, until the cheese bubbles. Serve with Cocktail Tostadas and Cold Green Chile Sauce. They should be eaten with tostadas rather than a fork. Serves 4-6.

BEAN & CHEESE CROQUETTES

2 cups mashed pinto beans
2 tb. grated onion
¼ tsp. dried oregano
¼ cup peeled green chiles, chopped
¼ cup Parmesan cheese
¼ tsp. MSG
½ tsp. salt
¼ lb. Monterey Jack cheese
1 egg
1 tb. water
bread crumbs
hot fat

Mash the beans and add onion, oregano, chiles, Parmesan cheese, salt and MSG. Cut the Monterey Jack into 12 cubes and make the each croquette with a piece of cheese in the middle. The cheese should be completely covered with the bean mixture. Roll each croquette in bread crumbs. Beat the egg with the water and dip each croquette into the mixture, then into bread crumbs again. Fry in deep fat until they are quite brown. Serve with Cold Green Chile Sauce (see p. 98). Serves 4.

Note: Fry one croquette first to see how long it takes: the cheese will not have melted inside until they are brown on the outside.

PUREE OF GARBANZOS

1 lb. dried garbanzos (chick-peas)
1 onion
2 carrots
2 slices of bacon
3 cups beef broth
1 bay leaf

one sprig each of thyme,
    parsley and oregano, tied
    in a cheesecloth bag with
    the bay leaf
butter
salt to taste

Soak the garbanzos overnight in water. Drain and cover with the broth and vegetables and add the cheesecloth bag of herbs. Cook slowly for at least four hours—though they are best if cooked much longer until they are quite creamy.

When they are done remove the vegetables and the cheesecloth bag and puree through a food mill. Add salt to taste and as much butter as you wish. Return to a pan to warm, but be careful not to burn the bottom. Serve with a lump of butter on top. Serves 4-6.

Note: Prepared in this manner the garbanzos taste very much like chestnuts and are very much less expensive as well as more easily done.

GARBANZO & CHORIZO CASSEROLE

1 lb. dried garbanzos (chick-peas)
salt to taste
3 slices of bacon, diced
1 chopped green onion
1 chopped green pepper
2 pressed cloves of garlic
1 cup crumbled chorizo

1 cup tomato sauce
¼ tsp. ground cumin
¾ tb. chili powder
¾ cup pitted ripe olives
¼ cup minced lamb's-quarters
 (or parsley)

Soak the garbanzos overnight in water, drain, and cover with fresh water. Cook until very tender—at least 6 hours. Add salt to taste after the first 3 hours.

Fry the bacon and remove from pan, then add to the same fat the onion, green pepper and garlic and sauté 10 minutes. Remove from the pan.

Make the chorizo into walnut-size balls and sauté them in the pan until they are brown. Remove and place the onion-pepper mixture back in (removing fat in the pan if there is too much), add the tomato sauce, cumin and chili powder. Cook 5 minutes, then add the olives and lamb's-quarters.

Mix this with the drained garbanzos and ½ cup of the liquid the garbanzos were cooked in. Place in a casserole, top with the chorizo balls, cover, and bake at 375° for 30-45 minutes. Serves 4-6.

YELLOW RICE
WITH STUFFED GREEN CHILES

1 cup rice	4 tb. butter
2½ cups chicken broth	6 peeled green chiles
pinch of saffron	1 3-oz. package cream
salt to taste	cheese

Bring the broth to a boil and add rice, saffron and salt (if the broth is not too salty). Lower the heat, cover and simmer 20-25 minutes. Butter a shallow casserole with 1 tb. of butter and place the cooked rice in it. Stuff the chiles with cream cheese and lay them on top. Melt the other 3 tb. of butter and pour it over the chiles. Bake at 350° for 10-15 minutes. Serves 3-6.

GREEN RICE

3 green peppers	1 tsp. salt
⅓ cup parsley	1 cup rice
2 peeled green chiles	1 tb. butter
1½ cups chicken broth	pepitas

Grate the green peppers on fine blade of the grater so that the skin is left and can be discarded. Place the grated peppers, parsley and chiles into a measuring cup and press down. Add enough water to fill the cup. Place in a blender and whirl until smooth. Add this to a sauce pan with 1½ cups chicken broth. Bring to a boil, then add the rice, salt and butter. When it comes to a boil turn down the flame and cover. Simmer for 20 minutes, or until just tender and the liquid is absorbed. Serve sprinkled with pepitas. Serves 4-6.

RICE with guacamole

Boil rice in your favorite manner and when it is done pack into a well-buttered ring mold. Place the mold in a shallow pan of hot water and bake at 350° for 30 minutes. Unmold the ring onto a warm platter and spread it with guacamole (see p. 87). Garnish with parsley and serve.

WITH TOASTED PIÑON NUTS

Cook rice by your favorite method. When it is done add Tabasco sauce to taste and a lump of butter. Mix thoroughly. Sauté piñon nuts in butter till they are golden and mix them into the rice. Serve immediately garnished with parsley.

Note: Minced pimiento may also be mixed in with the piñon nuts, or chopped peeled green chiles.

WITH COCONUT

1½ cups rice	¼ cup butter
2¾ cups chicken stock	1 4-oz. package of grated
2 whole cloves	sweetened coconut

Bring the stock to a boil, then add rice, cloves, butter and coconut. Cover and turn the fire low. Simmer for 20-25 minutes, or until all the water is absorbed. Remove the cloves before serving. Serves 4-6.

Vegetables

SUMMER VEGETABLES

1 lb. summer squash, sliced
 thinly
3 scraped ears of corn
1 tomato, peeled, seeded
 and chopped
1 peeled green chile, diced
1 small onion, chopped

½ pressed clove of garlic
butter
pinch of ground coriander
¼ tsp. dried mint
1 tsp. salt
milk

Prepare all the vegetables and sauté for 5 minutes in butter. Add the coriander, mint and salt and cover the pan. Cook slowly for 20 minutes stirring occasionally to prevent burning. Cover with milk and simmer an hour. Serves 4-6.

Note: If you wish, you may dice one 3-oz. package of cream cheese and serve it over the veegtables—it should be partially melted before you bring it to the table on the hot vegetables.

MEXICAN PEAS

2 cups fresh green peas
  (or frozen)
½ tsp. ground coriander
salt to taste

pinch of sugar
¼ cup finely chopped onion
1 tb. bacon fat

Cook the peas in boiling water with the coriander, salt and sugar until they are barely tender. Meanwhile, fry the onion gently in bacon fat until it is transparent. Drain the peas and add them to the onion. Cook for 5 minutes longer and serve. Serves 4.

MEXICAN GREEN BEANS

1 tb. bacon fat
¼ cup chopped onion
1 pressed clove of garlic
½ cup tomatoes, peeled,
  seeded and diced

pinch of nutmeg
¼ tsp. chili powder
salt to taste
1 package frozen green beans

Sauté onion and garlic in the bacon fat for 5 minutes, then add tomatoes, nutmeg, chili powder and salt. When it comes to the boil add the green beans. Simmer, covered, for 10-15 minutes. Serves 4.

STUFFED CHILES WITH CHEESE
NUMBER ONE

6 peeled green chiles	2 tb. flour
¼ lb. sharp cheddar cheese	pinch of salt
½ cup flour	hot fat
2 eggs, separated	

Slice the cheese and stuff each chile, then roll in flour. Beat the whites of the eggs until stiff, then fold in the yolks. Sift the flour with the salt over the mixture and fold it in carefully. Place the egg-flour mixture on a platter. Place the chiles on top, one by one, turning to completely coat with the batter. Place each one, using a large slotted spoon, on a saucer and, with as much batter as possible clinging to it, slip into the hot fat. Turn them when they are gold on one side and fry on the other. Remove and serve with Cooked Green Chile Sauce (see Sauce Section). Serves 3-6.

Note: These can be made ahead, drained on absorbent paper, and re-heated in the following sauce:

¼ cup grated onion	1 cup chicken broth
1 pressed clove of garlic	salt to taste
1 tb. olive oil	pinch of black pepper
1 cup canned tomatoes, sieved	1 tsp. dried oregano
(or 3 tb. tomato paste)	

Sauté the onion and garlic in the olive oil, add the tomatoes, then add the rest of the ingredients. If you use tomato paste you will have to add a bit of water to the sauce. Cook for 10 minutes. When ready to serve the stuffed chiles, bring the sauce to a boil and put the chiles in it. Cover the pan and steam for 5 minutes, or until they puff up. You may also place them in the oven with the sauce poured over them until they puff.

NUMBER TWO

4 peeled green chiles
4 slices sharp cheddar cheese
4 eggs, separated
¼ cup flour

½ tsp. salt
butter
Cooked Green Chile Sauce
(see p. 98)

Stuff the chiles with cheese. Beat the egg whites stiff and then sift the flour mixed with salt over them. Fold into the egg whites. Beat the yolks till creamy and then also fold them into the whites. Place half of this mixture in a buttered casserole, place the stuffed chiles on top, then cover with the rest of the mixture. Bake at 400° until it begins to brown on top. Serve with sauce. Serves 4.

STUFFED CHILES

WITH BEANS

4 peeled green chiles
1 cup refried beans
flour
2 eggs, separated
2 tb. flour
pinch of salt

hot fat
⅓ cup light cream
½ cup sharp cheddar,
  grated
Cooked Green Chile Sauce
  (see p. 98)

Stuff each chile with beans, then roll in flour. Make a batter, and fry the chiles, as in Stuffed Chiles With Cheese. Remove to a shallow baking dish, pour the cream over, then sprinkle with the grated cheese. Bake at 375° until the cheese melts and the cream starts to bubble. Serve with Cooked Green Chile Sauce. Serves 4.

WITH PICADILLO

Stuff chiles with picadillo (see p. 35) and proceed as for Stuffed Chiles With Cheese.

LAMB'S-QUARTERS

2 lb. lamb's-quarters
1 tsp. bacon fat (or butter)
¼ cup chopped onion

1 peeled green chile, chopped
salt to taste
pinch of sugar

Discard tough stems of the lamb's-quarters. Drop tender stems and leaves into boiling salted water and cook a few minutes until just tender. Drain in a sieve, pressing until all water is out. Sauté the onion in fat until it is transparent and then add the chile and cook a few minutes longer. Add the lamb's-quarters and cook until heated through. Serves 4.

Note: Spinach may be substituted for the lamb's-quarters.

SQUASH PANCAKES

WITH SQUASH BLOSSOMS

2 cups grated summer squash
(or zucchini)
½ cup flour
1 tsp. baking powder
½ tsp. salt
1 beaten egg

2 tb. minced parsley
2 drops Tabasco sauce
butter
1 clove of garlic
squash flowers

Grate the squash into a bowl and sift the flour, baking powder and salt onto it. Mix gently and then add the egg, the parsley and Tabasco sauce. Mix again. Fry these in butter as you would pancakes, each 3″ in diameter. In another pan sauté a clove of garlic in butter until it turns brown, then remove from pan. Flatten the squash flowers with a large knife and quickly sauté them. Serve the pancakes topped with the squash flowers. Serves 4-6.

CORN AND GREEN CHILES

1 package frozen corn	½ pressed clove of garlic
2 tb. olive oil	salt to taste
3 peeled green chiles, chopped	pinch of black pepper
	pinch of sugar

Cook corn in water just until thawed. Heat the olive oil in a frying pan and add the drained corn, garlic, green chiles, and other ingredients. Cover, and cook slowly for 15 minutes. It may be neccessary to add water during cooking if mixture seems too dry. Serves 4.

CORN FRITTERS

1 cup corn	1½ tsp. baking powder
2 peeled green chiles, chopped	½ tsp. salt
1 tb. pimiento, chopped	¼ tsp. powdered red chile
¼ cup corn meal	2 eggs, separated
1 cup flour	½ cup milk
	butter

Place the corn, chiles and pimiento into a bowl, add the corn meal, then sift flour, baking powder, salt and powdered red chile over the corn, etc. Separate the eggs and add the yolks to the corn-flour mixture. Mix thoroughly. Add the milk and mix again. Whip the egg whites till stiff and fold into the mixture. Fry in butter until golden on both sides. Serves 4-6.

GREEN CORN CAKES

6 ears of corn	1 tsp. chili powder
½ cup milk	(optional)
3 eggs, separated	oil
½ tsp. salt	

Slice corn off the cob and add the milk beaten with egg yolks. Mix thoroughly. Whip the egg whites with salt, until they are stiff and fold them into the corn mixture. Fry in a frying pan with a little oil, as you would pancakes. Serves 4-6.

CORNMEAL SOUFFLE
WITH CHEESE AND GREEN CHILE

3 cups milk, scalded	3-4 peeled green chiles,
1 cup white cornmeal	chopped
1 tsp. salt	½ cup Monterey Jack cheese,
1 tsp. bacon fat	grated
1 tsp. sugar	3 eggs, separated

Scald the milk. When bubbles begin to form around the edge, add the cornmeal slowly, beating with a wire whisk. Continue beating and scraping the bottom of the pan while it cooks slowly for 5 minutes. Add the salt, bacon fat, and sugar and cook for several minutes longer.

Remove from the fire and add the chiles, cheese and egg yolks. Combine thoroughly. Whip the whites till stiff, but not dry, and fold them into the cornmeal mixture.

Heat the oven to 350° and place a bit of bacon fat into a casserole, then place casserole in oven. When the fat has melted, remove and place the soufflé mixture in. Bake for 45 minutes, or until puffed up and beginning to brown on top. Serve with butter. Serves 4-6.

Note: This is actually a Southern spoonbread adapted by the Southwest, and like all spoonbread it is excellent. It is a good substitution for beans or rice with any meat dish.

AVOCADO SLICES

MARINATED WITH RUM

2 avocados, peeled, seeded and sliced	1 pressed clove of garlic
½ cup olive oil	¼ tsp. salt
3 tb. white wine vinegar	pinch of MSG
2 tb. rum	lettuce leaves

Place the sliced avocados in a shallow glass dish. Pour the oil, vinegar, rum, etc. over them and marinate, covered, for at least 4 hours in the refrigerator. Serve on lettuce leaves with the marinade poured over. Serves 4.

WITH PAPAYA

lettuce leaves	⅓ cup olive oil
1 papaya, peeled and sliced	4 fresh mint leaves, chopped
2 avocados, peeled, seeded and sliced	pinch of sugar
	pinch of black pepper
¼ cup lime juice	salt to taste

Place the lettuce on salad plates and place the papaya and avocados decoratively on the lettuce. Mix the other ingredients into a salad dressing and pour over the fruit. Serves 4.

Note: When papaya is not available I find that tangerine or orange sections make good substitutes.

WITH LIME

Halve and seed avocados. Sprinkle each half with salt and place on a leaf of lettuce. Serve with lime wedges.

WITH GREEN BEANS

2 cups French-cut green beans
1 avocado, peeled, seeded
  and sliced
2 pimientos cut into strips

1 Spanish onion sliced
  very thinly
French dressing
lettuce leaves

Cook the green beans, drain, and set in refrigerator to chill. Then toss all the ingredients together, being careful not to break up the avocado slices. Serve on lettuce leaves. Serves 4-6.

GUACAMOLE

2 avocados, peeled and seeded
juice of half a lemon
4 finely chopped green onions
1 tomato, peeled, seeded and
  diced finely
½ pressed clove of garlic

2 drops Tabasco sauce
½ tsp. chili powder
¼ tsp. MSG
pinch of sugar
½ tsp. salt

Mash avocados and sprinkle with lemon juice. Add all the other ingredients and mix thoroughly. Cover and chill in the refrigerator for 30 minutes to an hour. Serve on lettuce with cocktail tostadas stuck in it. The guacamole should be eaten with the tostadas. Serves 4.

Note: Dry white wine, or lime juice, or a mild white wine vinegar can be substituted for the lemon juice.

HOT AVOCADO SALAD

2 large tomatoes, peeled and
   cut into eighths
2 avocados, peeled, seeded
   and sliced
4 green onions, chopped
5 radishes, sliced

2 slices bacon, diced
1½ tb. white wine vinegar
1 tsp. chili powder
pinch of sugar
salt to taste
lettuce leaves

Prepare all the vegetables. Fry bacon, and when it is crisp remove to drain on absorbent paper. Add the vinegar, chili powder, sugar and salt to the bacon fat left in the pan and let it boil a minute on medium heat. Add all the vegetables to the pan and toss quickly and carefully, then immediately serve on lettuce leaves with the bacon sprinkled on top. Serves 4.

Note: This is a splendid variation on the Midwestern wilted lettuce salad, and makes a lunch in itself served with plenty of Cocktail Tostadas (see p. 9).

AVOCADO MOUSSE

3-4 avocados (2 cups of
  pulp)
3 tb. lemon juice
1 envelope gelatine
½ cup chicken broth
1 tb. onion juice
2 tb. finely chopped chives

salt to taste
3-4 drops Tabasco sauce
¾ cup heavy cream,
  whipped
¼ tsp. dry mustard
½ cup mayonnaise
1 tsp. olive oil

Sieve the avocados and measure to make 2 cups. Squeeze the lemon juice over it. Soak the gelatine in half of the chicken broth. Add the onion juice, chives, salt and Tabasco sauce to the avocado. Heat the other half of the broth to boiling and add the gelatine to it, off the fire. Stir until the gelatine is dissolved. Cool in the refrigerator.

Whip the cream, then add dry mustard to the mayonnaise and fold this into the cream. Add the gelatine to the avocado mixture, then also fold this into the cream. Oil a one quart mold lightly and turn the mousse into the mold. Chill for 5 hours, or until set.

Serves 6. Serve with this dressing:

⅓ cup wine vinegar
juice of 1 lemon
1 tsp. grated lemon rind
½ cup olive oil

pinch of paprika
pinch of black pepper
pinch of sugar
salt to taste

AVOCADO & TOMATO MOLD

AVOCADO ASPIC

1 envelope gelatine	½ cup sour cream
¼ cup cold water	½ cup mayonnaise
1 cup boiling water	1 tsp. salt
1 tsp. sugar	pinch of black pepper
2 tb. lemon juice	2 drops Tabasco sauce
1 cup sieved avocado	

Soften gelatine in cold water, then pour in the boiling water and stir until dissolved. Add sugar and 1 tb. of lemon juice. Chill this until slightly thickened, then mash avocado and add the other tb. lemon juice, sour cream, mayonnaise and other ingredients. Mix the two thoroughly and pour into a 2 quart mold, chill until set.

TOMATO ASPIC

1 envelope gelatine	½ tsp. sugar
¼ cup cold water	1 tb. lemon juice
1¾ cups boiling tomato juice	¼ tsp. salt
	dash of Worcestershire sauce

Soften gelatine in cold water, then pour in the boiling tomato juice and stir until dissolved. Add the other ingredients and let cool. Then pour over firm avocado aspic and chill until set. Unmold on a bed of lettuce. Serves 6.

CAULIFLOWER
FROSTED WITH GUACAMOLE

1 large cauliflower
½ cup olive oil
⅓ cup white wine vinegar
  (or ¼ cup lemon juice)
½ tsp. powdered red chile
pinch of sugar

1 tsp. salt
lettuce
guacamole (see p. 87)
sliced radishes
almonds, blanched, slivered
  and toasted

Cook head of cauliflower until the bottom core can be pierced with a fork. Make a dressing of the oil, vinegar, red chile, sugar and salt and pour this over the cauliflower, placed head down in a casserole or glass dish. Cover and cool in the refrigerator for several hours, turning several times. To serve, place the cauliflower on a bed of lettuce and spoon some of the dressing over it, then cover completely with guacamole. Decorate with sliced radishes and toasted almonds. Serves 4.

SALAD GREENS
WITH PIÑON & GREEN CHILE DRESSING

mixed salad greens	2 tb. peeled green chiles,
6 green onions, chopped	minced
½ cup piñon nuts	1 tb. olive oil
1 tbs. butter	salt to taste
½ tsp. salt	pinch of sugar
½ cup mayonnaise	¼ tsp. MSG
1 tb. lemon juice	¼ tsp. dried oregano
½ pressed clove of garlic	⅛ tsp. ground coriander

Wash and drain lettuce, tearing in bite-size pieces. Chop the green onions and add to the lettuce. Sauté the piñon nuts slowly in butter until they are golden, then remove and drain on absorbent paper. Sprinkle with salt. Combine the rest of the ingredients into a salad dressing, add to the greens and onions, and toss lightly. Then, just before serving, sprinkle the piñon nuts over the top of the salad.

WITH AVOCADO DRESSING

1 avocado,	¼ cup sour cream
peeled and seeded	½ tsp. salt
1 pressed clove of garlic	½ tsp. chili powder
1 tb. lime juice	pinch of sugar
1 tsp. white wine	mixed salad greens

Mash the avocado and pressed garlic thoroughly together, then add all the other ingredients, except the salad greens, and mix again. Place in a covered container in the refrigerator for at least 15 minutes, to chill, then toss with the salad greens.

WITH CHILI CROUTONS

3 slices of white bread   1 tsp. chili powder
3 tb. butter   salt to taste
1 clove of garlic   mixed salad greens

Trim crust from the bread and cut it into small cubes. Melt butter in the frying pan and cook the clove of garlic in it until it is brown, then remove. Add the chili powder and salt and then the bread cubes. Quickly toss the bread until all cubes are coated with the butter. Then remove and place on a cookie sheet in a 350° oven. Cook for 10 minutes, or until they are golden brown. Toss salad greens with your favorite dressing and at the last minute add the croutons.

GREEN CHILE SALAD

8 green peppers, or green chiles	salt to taste
⅔ cup olive oil	pinch of black pepper
⅓ cup red wine vinegar	pinch of sugar
	pimiento strips

Peel peppers or chiles (see Ingredients & Methods). Quarter each and cover with olive oil, vinegar, salt, pepper and sugar. Chill in the refrigerator for several hours, then drain and serve on lettuce leaves decorated with strips of pimiento. Serves 4.

STUFFED GREEN CHILE SALAD

12 peeled green chiles	salt to taste
¼ cup red wine vinegar	pinch of black pepper
⅓ cup olive oil	1 pressed clove of garlic
1 tsp. salt	½ tsp. dried basil
2 avocados, peeled, seeded and sliced	pinch of sugar
	12 lettuce leaves
1 cup summer squash, diced	seedless ripe olives

Marinate the chiles in vinegar, olive oil and salt for several hours. Mash the avocados and add 1 tb. of the marinade. Cook the squash until just tender in a bit of water, with the salt, pepper, garlic, basil and sugar.

When you wish to serve the salad, remove the chiles from the marinade and stuff them with the avocados mixed with the squash. Place on lettuce leaves and decorate with slices of seedless ripe olives. Pour any remaining marinade over the salad. Serves 4-6.

SQUASH SALAD

2 cups chopped green onions
4 cups thinly sliced summer squash (or zucchini)
3 green peppers, grated
3 avocados, peeled, seeded and sliced
3 tb. olive oil

2 tb. vinegar
1 tsp. dried basil
salt to taste
pinch of black pepper
pinch of sugar
lettuce leaves

Cook onions and squash in very little water until they are just tender. Drain and mix with the other vegetables. Combine the rest of the ingredients and pour over the vegetables. Chill thoroughly and serve on lettuce leaves. Serves 6.

TOMATO STUFFED
WITH CELERY AND PIÑON NUTS

Take small garden tomatoes and place each for a minute in boiling water. Then peel: the skin will slip off easily. Remove a slice from the top of each tomato and take out the seeds and pulp. Sprinkle the inside with salt and invert on absorbent paper. Let stand for half an hour. Mix very finely chopped celery and piñon nuts in a three-to-one proportion, with good mayonnaise. Fill the tomatoes and garnish with parsley.

GREEN GARBANZO SALAD

1 cup cooked (or canned)
  garbanzos (see p. 74)
3 chopped green onions
1 tb. minced parsley
1 peeled green chile, chopped
2-3 canned tomatillos,
  chopped (optional)
1 green pepper, grated
1 pressed clove of garlic

salt to taste
pinch of black pepper
pinch of sugar
1 tsp. ground coriander
  soaked in 1 tb. hot water
1 tsp. grated lemon peel
1 tb. olive oil
1 tb. tarragon vinegar
dash of seasoning salt

Combine all the ingredients (the water should be drained from the coriander and added). Refrigerate, covered, for several hours before serving. Serves 4.

ROOSTER'S BILL

6 oranges, peeled and sliced
Tabasco sauce
juice of half a lemon

salt
6 chopped green onions
chili powder

Prepare oranges and place 1-2 drops Tabasco sauce on each slice, then lay the slices on a large platter and sprinkle with the lemon juice and salt. Cover with foil and chill in the refrigerator for an hour or more. When ready to serve sprinkle each orange slice with chili powder and sprinkle with the chopped green onion. Serves 4.

Note: This is best served as a relish with meat, but also is good served on lettuce leaves, or in a cocktail cup, as a salad or a first course.

Sauces

RED CHILE SAUCE

RED CHILE PASTE

Take either fresh or dried red chiles, first wash them and break off the stems, then place in a pan of cold water and boil slowly for about 45 minutes. Remove from the fire and drain. When they are cool enough to handle, slip the skins off with rubber gloves on your hands (they burn). Then, also with gloves on, squeeze any seeds out. Return the chiles to the same water they were cooked in and cook about 15 minutes longer. Then run them through a food mill to puree. Add enough water in which they were cooked to make the puree the consistency of thick gravy, and add salt to taste. This can be frozen.

SAUCE

1 cup red chile paste (or ⅓ cup powdered red chile mixed with 1 tb. flour)
2 tb. bacon fat
½ cup grated onion

1 pressed clove of garlic
½ tsp. dried oregano
pinch of sugar
salt to taste

Prepare the chile paste. Then fry onion and garlic in the bacon fat until the onion is transparent. Add the pulp (or chile powder and flour with enough water to make a thin sauce). Add the other ingredients and cook for 30 minutes, or until the sauce has cooked down and thickened.

97

GREEN CHILE SAUCE

COLD

3 tomatoes, peeled, seeded and chopped (or 1 can of tomatoes)
½ cup chopped green onions
1 pressed clove of garlic
2 tb. chopped parsley
¼ cup peeled green chiles, chopped

2 pickled jalapeño peppers, seeded and minced
1 tsp. ground coriander soaked in 1 tb. hot water
½ tsp. salt
pinch of black pepper
pinch of sugar

Chop all the vegetables, drain the water from the coriander and add it, then combine all the ingredients. Chill at least an hour before serving.

Note: This sauce keeps well in the refrigerator in a covered jar. One tb. chopped lamb's-quarters may be added to the sauce if you wish.

COOKED

½ cup chopped green onions
1 pressed clove of garlic
2 tb. olive oil
2 tomatoes, peeled, seeded and chopped (or ½ cup canned tomatoes)
1 tb. chopped parsley

¼ cup peeled green chiles, chopped
1 tsp. ground coriander soaked in 1 tb. hot water
salt to taste
pinch of black pepper
1 whole clove

Sauté onion and garlic in olive oil until the onion is transparent. Add the tomatoes, chiles, parsley, the water drained from the coriander and the rest of the ingredients. Simmer for 10-15 minutes.

CHILE MEAT SAUCE

1½ lbs. ground beef
1 cup chopped onion
2 pressed cloves of garlic
2 tb. bacon fat
1½ cup canned tomatoes, with
juice from the can
(or ½ cup tomato sauce,
or 4 tb. tomato paste)

½ cup canned beef bouillon,
undiluted
3-4 tb. chili powder
1 tsp. each sugar and salt
1 cup water
¼ tsp. ground cumin
½ tsp. dried oregano

Sauté ground beef in frying pan, and when it is brown remove from the pan and drain on absorbent paper to remove the excess fat. Remove any fat from pan and place the bacon fat in it, then sauté the onion and garlic in fat until the onion is transparent. Add the cooked meat to the onions, and the tomatoes which have been put through a food mill with the juice from the can (or tomato sauce or tomato paste). Add the rest of the ingredients and simmer for about 2 hours. If it gets too dry add more water. Taste for salt and add more if you wish during the last half hour of cooking.

FRANCES SOMMER'S

2½ lbs. ground round
3 tb. olive oil
4 pressed cloves of garlic
1 tbs. chili powder
½ tsp. dried oregano
½ tsp. ground cumin
½ tsp. dried sweet basil

2 tb. white wine
1 7-oz. can green chile salsa
2 tb. tomato paste
1½ cups chicken broth
½ tsp. MSG
salt to taste

Sauté the meat with the garlic in olive oil. Add the rest of the ingredients and cook for 1½-2 hours, or until the sauce is cooked down and thickened.

MOLE SAUCE

NUMBER ONE

2 green peppers	½ tsp. cinnamon
1 tsp. anise seed	1 tsp. salt
2 tb. sesame seed	½ tsp. ground coriander
5 cloves of garlic	2 oz. grated bitter chocolate
¾ cup almonds	2 tb. powdered red chile
3 minced tortillas	½ cup oil
6 large tomatoes, peeled, seeded and chopped	2 cups chicken broth (or turkey)
pinch of ground cloves	

Grind the peppers, anise, sesame, garlic, almonds, tortillas and tomatoes. Mix into a paste and add all the spices. Place the oil in a frying pan and add the mixture to it. Fry for several minutes, then add the stock and simmer until quite thick.

NUMBER TWO (QUICK METHOD)

½ cup grated onion	2 tsp. chili powder
2 pressed cloves of garlic	pinch of allspice
2 tb. oil	1 2-oz. can mole poblano powder
2 tomatoes peeled and seeded (fresh or canned)	2 cups chicken broth

Sauté the onion and garlic in oil until the onion is transparent. Add the tomatoes which you have put through a food mill and simmer for 5 minutes. Add the spices, mole powder and chicken broth and simmer about 15 minutes, or until thick. This can cook longer if you wish, as further cooking improves the flavor, and more stock can be added if necessary. The sauce should be the consistency of thick cream.

JALAPEÑO SAUCE
FRANCES SOMMER'S

6 pickled jalapeño peppers	6 chopped green onions
½ tsp. salt	2 tb. chopped parsley
1 tb. olive oil	pinch of sugar
1 tb. lemon juice (or lime)	1 tomato, peeled, seeded
½ tsp. Worcestershire sauce	and chopped (optional)

Slice the jalapeños lengthwise, remove seeds, then mince finely. Combine with the rest of the ingredients and let stand for at least an hour before serving.

Note: One tb. white wine is a good addition to this sauce.

PIÑON & PARSLEY SAUCE

½ cup minced parsley	¼ cup olive oil
½ cup chopped piñon nuts	salt to taste
2 tb. lemon (or lime) juice	pinch of sugar
1 tsp. pickled jalapeño pepper,	¼ tsp. MSG
seeded and minced	

Combine all ingredients and serve cold over shrimp, fish, cold roast beef, cauliflower, etc.

CHILE BLEU CHEESE SAUCE

2 tb. chili powder	2 tb. bleu cheese
1 tb. minced green onions	salt to taste
1 tb. olive oil	1 cup beer (or orange juice)

Mix the first ingredients thoroughly, then add the beer. Serve with meat or fish.

Desserts

FLAN

¾ cup sugar	4 eggs	pinch of salt
3 cups milk	½ cup sugar	1 tsp. vanilla extract

Melt ¾ cup sugar in a saucepan until there are no lumps and it is a deep amber color. Immediately remove from fire and pour into custard cups or a baking dish. While it is still liquid tip the cups or dish in all directions quickly so that the sugar coats the sides and bottom. Scald the milk, and when bubbles begin to come to the sides, remove from the fire.

Beat the eggs until frothy and then stir in the ½ cup sugar, salt and vanilla. Add the scalded milk slowly, beating constantly, then pour through a sieve into the cups or baking dish. Set in a pan with about 1" of hot water in it and bake at 325° for an hour or more.

When it is done a knife inserted at the center should come out clean. Custard cups will take less time to cook than a whole custard. Remove to a rack, and when it has cooled, place it, covered, in the refrigerator for several hours.

To unmold, run a knife about the edge and then invert into plate or plates. If you bake as a whole custard place your platter over the dish after you have run a knife about the edge of the custard and quickly lift both together and invert. Serves 6.

PUMPKIN FLAN

1 cup sugar	⅔ cup sugar
2 cups light cream	1 tsp. salt
1 cup milk	½ cup rum
2 cups strained pumpkin	6 eggs

Melt 1 cup sugar over a low flame until there are no lumps and it is a deep amber color. Immediately remove from the fire and pour it into your baking dish. While it is still liquid tip the dish in all directions quickly so that the sugar coats the sides and bottom. Scald the cream with the milk, and when bubbles begin to come to the sides add the ⅔ cup sugar, pumpkin, salt and rum. Remove from the fire and beat the eggs till frothy. Pour a bit of the pumpkin mixture into the eggs and beat again. Then add the eggs to the pumpkin, beating constantly. Pour this into the caramelized baking dish and put it in a pan in which there is about 1″ of hot water. Bake it at 350° for an hour, or until a knife inserted into the center comes out clean. Allow to cool and invert on a serving dish. Serves 6.

Note: This can be served chilled, or, as I prefer it, still warm and flaming with rum. To do this, invert after it has cooled a bit and let it stand for about 10 minutes. Pour off the caramel syrup that has accumulated around the edge into a sauceboat. Warm ⅓ cup rum and pour over the flan and ignite with a match. Keep spooning the rum onto the top as it burns to make sure the flame burns itself out, then serve with the additional caramel syrup separately.

COCONUT FLAN

1 cup sugar	2 egg yolks
¾ cup cornstarch	2 cups flaked coconut
1 tsp. salt	1 tsp. grated orange rind
2 cups milk	2 tsp. vanilla extract
2 cups light cream	

Sift sugar, cornstarch and salt into a double boiler, then add the milk and cream, beating with a wire whisk until smooth. Cook over boiling water until thickened, stirring occasionally to keep smooth. Beat the egg yolks in a bowl and gradually add the hot mixture, beating constantly.

Return to the double boiler and cook, stirring steadily, for a few minutes. Cool. Beat with an eggbeater for 2 minutes, then fold in the coconut, orange rind and vanilla. Pour into custard cups and chill. Serve with whipped cream sweetened with powdered sugar. Serves 6.

BANANAS
GLAZED WITH GUAVA-RUM

½ cup guava jelly   3 tb. butter
2 tb. rum (or tequila) 1 tsp. brown sugar
6 ripe bananas   pinch of salt

Melt the jelly with the rum over a slow fire and let it simmer a few minutes until it thickens to a glazing consistency. Slice the bananas lengthwise. Melt the butter in a frying pan and sauté the bananas, first on one side, then the other. After you first turn the bananas sprinkle the sugar and the barest pinch of salt over them, and cook just until they begin to brown. Place on warm plates and glaze with the guava-rum mixture. Serves 6.

WITH RUM AND WHIPPED CREAM

6 bananas   ½ cup whipping cream
4 tb. butter   ¼ cup powdered sugar
½ cup sugar   ¼ tsp. vanilla extract
½ cup rum

Peel bananas, slice lengthwise and fry in butter. Remove to a serving dish. Add sugar to rum in saucepan. Cook slowly till the sugar is dissolved, then pour over the bananas. Marinate, covered, for several hours in the refrigerator. Serve with whipped cream flavored with sugar and vanilla. Serves 6.

ALMENDRADO

1 tb. gelatine	½ tsp. almond extract
½ cup cold water	½ tsp. vanilla extract
1 cup boiling water	red and green vegetable
1 cup sugar	coloring (optional)
5 egg whites	chopped, toasted almonds

Soak the gelatine in cold water, then add the boiling water and stir until the gelatine is dissolved. Add the sugar and continue stirring until the sugar is also dissolved. Chill in the refrigerator until it begins to stiffen, then remove and beat with an egg-beater until it is frothy. Keep cool while you beat the egg whites stiff, then fold the whites very thoroughly with the almond and vanilla extracts and the gelatine mixture.

If you wish you can divide the gelatine-egg-white mixture into thirds and color ⅓ red, ⅓ green and leave the other as is. Pour first one color, then the next into a glass loaf pan and chill. To serve, slice the dessert and pour over custard sauce and garnish with chopped toasted almonds.

CUSTARD SAUCE

2 cups milk	½ tsp. vanilla extract
5 egg yolks	½ tsp. almond extract
¼ cup sugar	1 cup of whipping cream
pinch of salt	(optional)

Scald the milk. Beat the egg yolks, then add water and sugar. Add a few tablespoons of hot milk to egg yolks, mixing well, then add remainder of milk. Put egg-milk mixture in top of double boiler over simmering water. Cook, stirring constantly until the custard coats the spoon. Remove from fire, and add flavorings. Chill. If you wish, before serving, you can fold in one cup of whipped cream.

(If cooked too quickly over open flames or unit, or over rapidly boiling water, custard will curdle.)

COCONUT & ALMOND DESSERT

1 cup sugar
1 cup water
1 4-oz. can grated coconut
1 stick of cinnamon

1 *whole clove*
4 *beaten egg yolks*
butter
½ *cup slivered, toasted almonds*

Boil the sugar in water for about 10 minutes, or until it begins to make a syrup, then add the coconut, cinamon stick, and the clove. Simmer, stirring often, for about 15 minutes. Cool slightly and place a bit of the mixture into the beaten eggs, stir, and place the rest of the mixture in bit by bit.

Place over medium heat, stirring constantly, and cook until the mixture begins to make a ball and lift off the bottom of the pan. Pour into a buttered shallow baking dish in which you can serve the dessert. Place under a broiler until it turns a golden brown. Remove from the oven and sprinkle with almonds, then chill in the refrigerator. Serves 4-6.

Note: This can also be removed whole from the baking dish and carefully placed on a dessert platter for serving.

MANGOES

IN ORANGE SAUCE

½ cup sugar
¼ cup water
juice of half an orange
grated peel of half an orange

3 tb. orange liqueur
6 peeled halves of mangoes
(or 6 canned halves)

Combine the sugar, water, orange juice, grated peel and the liqueur in a saucepan and cook until it makes a syrup, then remove from fire and pour over the mangoes. Refrigerate, covered, for 24 hours. Serves 6.

Note: These can be eaten as is, or, for a more substantial dessert, be served over vanilla ice-cream.

MANGO FLOATING ISLAND

3 eggs
¼ cup sugar
pinch of salt
2 cups scalded milk
1 tb. sherry

1 can of mangoes
½ cup whipping cream
¼ tsp. vanilla extract
powdered sugar

Beat the eggs until they are light, then add the sugar, salt and, bit by bit, the scalded milk. Cook, stirring constantly in a double boiler over very hot but not boiling water until the custard coats a spoon. This will take 7 minutes, or more. Add sherry and let the mixture cool. Drain juice from the mangoes and slice them. Place them in the bottom of a glass serving dish and top with the custard. Chill in the refrigerator. To serve, top with whipped cream flavored with the vanilla and as much powdered sugar as you wish. Serves 4-6.

MANGO ICE CREAM

NUMBER ONE

Mangoes to make 1 lb. of puree   ⅓ cup sugar
2 cups whipping cream   pinch of salt

Puree mangoes, then whip cream and fold in sugar and salt. Carefully fold the puree into the cream and freeze. Serves 6.

NUMBER TWO

1 large can of mangoes   1 cup whipping cream
(6 halves)   pinch of salt

Blend drained mangoes in blender, then whip cream and fold in the mango puree with salt. Add enough syrup from the can to bring to desired sweetness. You may also add extra sugar if you wish. Freeze. Serves 6.

ICE CREAM

MEXICAN CHOCOLATE

1 oz. bitter chocolate	3 egg whites, beaten
¼ tsp. cinnamon	1½ tsp. vanilla
⅔ cup sugar	2 cups whipping cream
¾ cup water	

Grate chocolate and blend with cinnamon. Heat the sugar with water and bring to boiling point, then cook without stirring for 5 minutes. Beat whites of the eggs stiff and gradually beat the sugar syrup into them until the mixture cools. Fold in the chocolate-cinnamon mixture, the vanilla and, lastly, the cream which you have whipped. Freeze in ice-cube trays in the refrigerator. Serves 6.

AVOCADO

1 tsp. gelatine	¼ cup lemon juice (or lime)
1 tb. cold water	¾ cup sugar
1 cup milk	pinch of salt
2 avocados, peeled and seeded	1 cup whipping cream

Soften the gelatine in cold water. Heat the milk just until bubbles start around the edge, then dissolve the gelatine in it. Set aside to cool while you prepare the avocados. Sieve avocados and add lemon juice. Beat the sugar in until it has dissolved, then add the milk-gelatine mixture. Beat. Whip the cream and fold it in. Freeze. Serves 6.

TEQUILA SHERBET

1½ cups sugar   ⅓ cup tequila
3 cups water   1 egg white
½ cup lime juice   ¼ tsp. salt
½ tsp. grated lime peel

Stir sugar and water together and boil for 5 minutes to make a syrup. During the last minute of cooking add the lime peel. Remove from the fire and stir in lime juice, then place in the freezing compartment of your refrigerator.

When it is frozen to a thick mush, remove and place the mixture in a blender. Add the tequila, egg white and salt and blend thoroughly.

Replace in the refrigerator and freeze. If this becomes too hard when you wish to serve it, or has ice crystals, simply whirl in the blender to soften it. Serves 4.

GUAVA PASTE
WITH CREAM CHEESE

Serve equal portions of guava paste and softened cream cheese.

Note: This is one of the simplest and most common desserts served after a Mexican meal in the Southwest: it is also difficult to improve upon. Guava paste may not be easy to find outside the Southwest, but it is well worth the effort of a special trip to your gourmet shop.

QUINCE CHEESE

5 lbs. quinces   5 lbs. sugar

Wash and core the quinces, remove the seeds, then quarter and cover with water. Cook until the fruit is soft. Pass through a food mill. Place in a large saucepan and add sugar. Cook until thick and dark red in color. Stir frequently to prevent burning. When done, pour into molds. After it cools, take out of the molds and cover with cheese cloth and set in the sun to dry. When it has dried thoroughly wrap in waxed paper and store. Serve with softened cream cheese.

CANDIED LIMES

2 dozen large limes   ½ tsp. salt
1½ cups sugar   juice of one lemon

Scrape each lime so the peel is roughened, but not removed. Then slash each one with a long vertical cut. Soak for 3 days in cold water to cover, and change the water two times a day. Each time you have changed the water squeeze each lime gently. On the third day boil the sugar, salt, lemon juice and ¾ cup water for a few minutes, then add the drained and squeezed limes. Simmer about 15-20 minutes, then remove from heat and let stand for 8 hours. Boil them again in the same syrup for another 15-20 minutes, then again let them stand for 8 hours and boil 15-20 minutes for the third time. The limes, finally, should be transparent.

AVOCADO SOUFFLÉ

butter	2 tb. lime juice
granulated sugar	1 tsp. vanilla extract
3 tb. flour	1 tb. rum
¾ cup milk	¾ cup sieved ripe
⅓ cup sugar	avocado
1 tsp. grated lime peel	pinch of salt
4 egg yolks	1 tb. sugar
2 tb. butter	

Preheat oven to 400°. Butter a 6-cup soufflé mold, then sprinkle with granulated sugar. Beat the flour in a saucepan with a bit of the milk until it is well blended. Then add the rest of the milk, the sugar and lime peel.

Stir over moderate heat until it comes to a boil, then cook stirring constantly for about 30 seconds longer. The sauce will be very thick.

Remove from the fire and cool slightly. Separate the eggs and beat the yolks into the sauce one by one, then add the butter, lime juice, vanilla, rum and sieved avocado. Add one more egg white to the others separated from the yolks, then beat with salt until soft peaks are formed. Sprinkle the sugar on and beat it until stiff. Fold the whites into the yolk-avocado mixture and turn it into the soufflé mold. Place in the oven and turn down heat to 375° immediately. Bake for 30-35 minutes. Serve, if you wish, with whipped cream slightly sweetened and flavored either with grated lime peel, or rum. Serves 6.

Menus

SUMMER LUNCHEONS

I.

Cocktail Tostadas (page 9)
Salad Greens with Avocado Dressing (page 92)
Cream Cheese and Green Pepper Pie (page 13)
Tequila Sherbet (page 111)

II.

Gazpacho (page 30)
Trout Frosted with Guacamole (page 16)
Rice with Toasted Piñon Nuts (page 77)
Mango Ice Cream #1 (page 109)

SUMMER SUPPERS

I.

Barbecued Hamburgers with Guacamole (page 46)
Summer Vegetables (page 78)
Hot Tortillas
Mexican Chocolate Ice Cream (page 110)

II.

Sour Cream Tostadas (page 63)
Green Salad with Chile Croutons (page 63)
Fresh Pineapple

III.

Cold Avocado Soup #2 (page 26)
Grilled Southwestern Shrimp (page 47)
Yellow Rice with Stuffed Green Chiles (page 76)
Mangoes in Orange Sauce (page 108)

SUMMER DINNER

Lyle's Jellied Garlic Soup (page 28)
Grilled Steak with Guacamole (page 46)
Refried Beans with Monterey Jack Cheese (page 71)
Cocktail Tostadas with Chili Powder (page 9)
Tomatoes Stuffed with Celery and Piñon Nuts (page 95)
Flan (page 102)

BRUNCHES

I.

Scrambled Eggs with Tortillas (page 21)
Rooster's Bill (page 96)

II.

Avocado and Papaya Salad (page 87)
Huevos Rancheros (page 20)
Refried Beans (page 71)

LUNCHEONS

I.

Avocado Slices Marinated in Rum (page 87)
Escabeche of Shrimp (page 16)
Mexican Chocolate Ice Cream (page 110)

II.

Pinto Bean Soup with Cheese (page 25)
Eggs with Chorizo (page 21)
Stuffed Green Chili Salad (page 94)
Mangoes in Orange Sauce (page 108)

SUPPERS

I.

Hot Avocado Salad (page 88)
Mexican Meatloaf (page 37)
Flan (page 102)

II.

Avocado Soup (page 26)
Beans with Bacon (page 72)
Mango Floating Island (page 108)

III.

Black Bean Soup with Tortillas (page 25)
Chicken Crepes with Green Chile Sauce, Emmanuel (page 60)
Mexican Peas (page 79)
Avocado with Lime (page 87)
Guava Paste with Cream Cheese (page 111)

DINNERS

I.

Avocado Enchiladas (page 55)
Porkchops & Kidney Beans (page 32)
Salad Greens with Piñon & Green Chile Dressing (page 92)
Guava Paste with Cream Cheese (page 111)

II.

Puree of Garbanzo Soup (page 27)
Chicken-Cheese Tamale Pie (page 48)
Salad Greens with Avocado Dressing (page 92)
Guava-Rum Glazed Bananas (page 105)

III.

Lyle's Jellied Garlic Soup (page 28)
Baked Pork Loin with Oranges (page 31)
Puree of Garbanzos (page 74)
Cold Cauliflower Frosted with Guacamole (page 91)
Tequila Sherbet (page 111)

IV.

Gazpacho (page 30)
Leg of Lamb with Chile Wine Sauce (page 34)
Banana Mole Enchiladas (page 58)
Refried Beans (page 71)
Avocado Ice Cream (page 110)

SPECIAL MEALS

COCKTAIL PARTY WITH GREEN HORS D'OEUVRES

Cocktail Tostadas (page 9)
Pepitas
Pickled Jalapeños Stuffed with Walnut Cheese (page 11)
Guacamole (page 87)
Green Garbanzo Salad (page 96)
Green Pepper Salad (page 94)

TYPICAL SOUTHWESTERN MEXICAN DINNER

Cheese Enchiladas with Meat Sauce (page 53)
Tacos (page 67)
Stuffed Chiles with Cheese (page 80)
Refried Beans (page 71)
Cold Green Chile Sauce (page 98)
Cocktail Tostadas (page 9)
Guacamole (page 87)
Flan (page 102)

SOUTHWESTERN
THANKSGIVING DINNER

Mexican Cashews (page 11)
Pickled Jalapeños Stuffed with Walnut Cheese (page 11)
Cocktail Tostadas Variation #2 (page 9)
Bean Dip #1 (page 10)
Avocado Soup (page 26)
Spiced Oysters (page 12)
Turkey with Puree or Garbanzo Stuffing (page 43)
Mexican Peas (page 79)
Rooster's Bill (page 96)
Pumpkin Flan (page 103)

Index

Almendrado, 106
Appetizers
  Bean Croquettes, 13
  Dips, 10
  Cocktail Tostadas, 9
  with Chili Powder, 9
  Variations, 9
  Cold Garbanzo Dip, 10
  Chile con Queso, 12
  Cream Cheese & Green Pepper Pie, 13
  Mexican Cashews, 11
  Pickled Jalapeños Stuffed with Walnut
  Cheese, 11
  Ripe Olives Stuffed with Green Chile,
  11
  Spiced Oysters, 12
Avocados, 3, 26, 55, 65, 86-89, 90, 94,
110, 113
Avocado Mousse, 89
Avocado Soups, 26
Avocado & Tomato Mold, 90
Aztec Pie, 59

Bananas, 58, 105
Barbecue
  Chicken, 47
  Hamburgers with Chile Meat Sauce,
  46
  with Guacamole, 46
  Lamb, 45
  Pork Chops, 45
  Spareribs, 44

Grilled Steaks, 46
  with Jalapeño Sauce, 46
  Veal, 45
Bean Croquettes, 13
Bean Dips, 10
Beans, 3, 10, 13, 25, 56, 64, 70, 71, 72,
73, 82
Beans, Fried & Refried, 71
  Variations, 71
Beans & Rice
  Bean & Cheese Croquettes, 73
  Beans, Pinto or Kidney, 70
  Fried & Refried, 71
  Variations, 71
  with Bacon, 72
  Garbanzo & Chorizo Casserole, 75
  Rice, Coconut, 77
  Rice, Green, 76
  with Guacamole, 7
  with Toasted Piñon Nuts, 7
  Yellow, Stuffed with Green Chiles, 76
  Garbanzos, Purée of, 74
Beef, 36
Black Bean Soup, 25
Burros, 62

Candied Limes, 112
Crab, Mexican Deviled, 17
Cashews, Mexican, 11
Cauliflower Frosted with Guacamole, 91
Cheese, 3
Cheese and Green Chile Cornmeal
Souffle, 85

Chicken Casserole with Green Chiles and Sour Cream, 42
Chicken-Cheese Tamale Pie, 48-49
Chicken Crepes with Green Chile Sauce, Emmanuel, 60
Chicken and Green Chile Pie, 59
Chicken with Green Chiles and Sour Cream, 42
Chicken with Pumpkinseed Sauce, 41
Chilaquiles, 39
Chile Bleu Cheese Sauce, 101
Chili con Carne, 38
Chile con Queso, 12
Chile Meatloaf Stuffed with Pinto Beans, 37
Chile Meat Sauce, 99
Chili Powder, 4
Chiles, 3-4
Chile Sauces, 4, 84, 92, 97, 98
Chiles, Stuffed, 76, 80, 81, 82
Chimichangas, 62
Chorizo, 4, 38, 64, 75
Corn & Green Chiles, 84
Corn Fritters, 84
Cream Cheese and Green Pepper Pie, 13

Desserts
  Almendrado, 106
  Avocado Ice Cream, 110
    Soufflé, 113
  Bananas Glazed with Guava & Rum, 105
    with Rum & Whipped Cream, 105
  Coconut & Almond Dessert, 107
  Flan, 102
    Coconut, 104
    Pumpkin, 103
  Guava Paste with Cream Cheese, 111
  Mango Floating Island, 108
    Ice Cream, 109
    in Orange Sauce, 108
  Mexican Chocolate Ice Cream, 110

Quince Cheese, 112
  Tequilla Sherbet, 111
Deviled Crab, 17

Eggs, 20, 21, 23
  with Chorizo, 21
  Scrambled, with Tortillas, 21
  in Spanish Tomato Sauce, 23
  Huevos Rancheros, 20
    with Refried Beans, 20
  Green Chile & Cheese Soufflé, 22
Enchiladas, 53-58
Escabeche of Shrimp, 16

Fish
  Fish Fillets with Chile & Wine Sauce, 15
  Mexican Deviled Crab, 17
  Escabeche of Shrimp, 16
  Red Snapper in Mexican Sauce, 18
  Seviche, 19
  Trout Frosted with Guacamole, 16
Flans, 102, 103, 104

Garbanzo & Chorizo Casserole, 75
Garbanzo Dip, Cold, 10
Garbanzos, 10, 27, 74, 75, 96
Garlic, 5
Garlic Soup, Lyle's Jellied, 28
Gazpacho, 30 (Texas?)
Green Beans, Mexican, 79
Green Chile Sauce, Cold, 98
Green Chile and Cheese Soufflé, 22
Green Corn Cakes, 85
Green Garbanzo Salad, 96
Guacamole, 87
Guava Paste with Cream Cheese, 111

Hamburgers, 46
Huevos Rancheros, 20

Jalapeños, 4
Jalapeño Sauce, Frances Sommers', 101
Jalapeños, Pickled, Stuffed with Walnut
  Cheese, 11

Lamb, 34, 45
Lamb's-Quarters, 5, 83
Leg of Lamb in Chile & Wine Sauce, 34

Mango Floating Island, 108
Mango Ice Cream, 109
Mangoes in Orange Sauce, 108
Masa Harina, 5
Meat
  Leg of Lamb in Chile & Wine Sauce,
  34
  Mexican Round Steak, 36
  Pork Chops & Kidney Beans, 32
  Pork Loin, Baked, with Oranges, 31
  Posole, 32
  Roast Beef, Cold, with Guacamole, 36
  Steaks, Grilled, with Guacamole, 36
  Stew with Squash Blossoms, 35
  Tinga, 33
  Meatball Soup, Mexican, 24
  Meatloaf, Mexican, 37
  Mole, 43, 58, 100

Olives Stuffed with Green Chile, 11
Onions, 5
Oysters, Spiced, 12

Peas, Mexican, 79
Pepitas, 7
Peppers, Green, 5
Picadillo, 35
Piñon & Parsley Sauce, 101
Piñon Nuts, 7
Pinto Bean Soup, 25
Pork, 31, 57
Pork Chops, 32, 45
Posole, 32

Poultry
  Chicken Casserole with Green Chiles,
  42
  Chicken, Fried, with Cold Green Chile
  Sauce, 40
    with Green Chiles & Sour Cream
    Mole, 43
    with Pumpkinseed Sauce, 41
  Turkey with Garbanzo Stuffing, 43
    Mole, 43
Puree of Garbanzo Soup, 27
Puree of Garbanzos, 74

Quesadillas, 60
  with Green Chile Sauce and
  Guacamole, 69
  with Picadillo, 11
  with Squash Flowers
Quince Cheese, 112

Red Snapper with Mexican Sauce, 18
Rice, 76, 77
Ripe Olives Stuffed with Green Chile,
  11
Rooster's Bill, 96

Salads
  Avocado Salad with Green Beans, 87
    Hot, 88
  Avocado with Lime, 87
    Mousse, 89
    with Papaya, 87
  Avocado & Tomato Mold, 90
  Avocado Slices Marinated with Rum,
  86
  Cauliflower Frosted with Guacamole,
  91
  Green Chile Salads, 1, 94
    Green Garbanzo Salad, 96
  Guacamole, 87
    Rooster's Bill, 96

Salad Greens with Avocado Dressing, 92
  with Chile Croutons, 93
  with Piñon & Green Chili Dressing, 92
  Squash Salad, 95
  Tomatoes Stuffed with Celery & Piñon Nuts, 95
Salad Greens with Avocado Dressing, 92
Salad Greens with Chili Croutons, 93
Salad Greens with Piñon & Green Chile Dressing, 92
Sauces, 97-101
  Chile Bleu Cheese, 101
    Green, cold, 98; cooked, 98
  Chile Meat Sauce, 99
    Frances Sommers', 99
    Red, 97
  Guacamole, 87
  Jalapeño Sauce, Frances Sommers', 101
  Mole Sauce, 100
  Piñon & Parsley Sauce, 101
Seviche 19
Shrimp, 16, 47
Souffles, 22
Soups
  Avocado, 26
  Black Bean with Tortillas, 25
  Gazpacho, 30
  Lyle's Jellied Garlic, 28
  Mexican Meatball, 24
  Mexican Summer, 29
  Pinto Bean, 25
  Puree of Garbanzo, 27
Spareribs, 44
Squash Blossoms, 6
Squash Pancakes with Squash Blossoms, 83
Squash Salad, 95
Steaks, 36, 46
Stew with Squash Blossoms, 35
Summer Soup, 29

Tabasco, 5
Tacos, 67
Tamale Pie, 6
Tamales and Tamale Pies
  Mixtures, 50
  Fillings: Chicken,51; Beef,51; Pork,52
  Chicken-Cheese Tamale Pies, 48-49
Tequila Sherbet, 111
Tinga, 33
Tomatillo, 7
Tomatoes, 7
Tomatoes Stuffed with Celery and Piñon Nuts, 95
Tortillas, 84
Tortillas & Dishes Using
  Aztec Pie, 59
  Burros, 60
  Chicken & Green Chile Pie, 59
  Chicken Crepes with Green Chile Sauce, Emmanuel, 61-62
  Chimichangas, 60
  Enchiladas with Green Chile Sauce, 54
    Avocado, 55
    Banana Mole, 58
    Bean, 56
    Cheese, 53
    Chicken Mole, 58
    Cream Cheese, 55
    Pork, 57
    Sour Cream, 54
  Quesadillas, 69
    with Green Chile Sauce, 69
    with Picadillo, 69
  Tacos, 67
    Chicken, with Tomatillo Sauce, 68
    with Tinga, 67
  Tostadas, 63
    Avocado, 65
    Cheese, with Flour Tortillas, 66
    with Meat Sauce, 66
    Chorizo, 64
    Sour Cream, Cynthia's, 63

with Refried Beans, 64
  Squash Flower, 65
Tostadas, 9, 63, 64, 65
Trout Frosted with Guacamole, 16
Turkey with Garbanzo Stuffing, 43
Turkey, Mole, 43

Veal, 45
Vegetables
  Cheese & Green Chile Cornmeal
  Soufflé, 85

Chiles, Stuffed with Beans, 82
  Stuffed with Cheese, 82
  Stuffed with Picadillo, 82
Corn Fritters, Southwestern, 84
Corn & Green Chiles, 84
Green Corn Cakes, 85
Lamb's-Quarters, 83
Mexican Green Beans, 79
Mexican Peas, 79
Squash Pancakes with Squash
  Blossoms, 83
Summer Vegetables, 78